Earth House Hold

EARTH HOUSE HOLD

Technical Notes & Queries
To Fellow Dharma Revolutionaries

Gary Snyder

A New Directions Book

Manufactured in the United States of America

New Directions Books are published for James Laughlin by New Directions Publishing Corporation, 333 Sixth Avenue, New York 10014.

FOR ODA SESSŌ RŌSHI (1901-1966)

"the mysterious further higher peak"

Contents

Contents

Earth House Hold

LOOKOUT'S JOURNAL

A. Crater Mountain

22 June 52   Marblemount Ranger Station
                    Skagit District, Mt. Baker National Forest

Hitchhiked here, long valley of the Skagit. Old cars parked in
the weeds, little houses in fields of bracken. A few cows, in
stumpland.

Ate at the "parkway café" real lemon in the pie
          "—why don't you get a jukebox in here"
          "—the man said we weren't important enough"

- - - -

28 June

                        Blackie Burns:
"28 years ago you could find a good place to fish.
GREEDY & SELFISH   NO RESPECT FOR THE
    LAND
           tin cans, beer bottles, dirty dishes
           a shit within a foot of the bed
one sonuvabitch out of fifty
fishguts in the creek
the door left open for the bear.

If you're takin forestry fellas keep away
from the recreation side of it:
first couple months you see the women you say
       'there's a cute little number'
the next three months it's only another woman
after that you see one coming out of the can
       & wonder if she's just shit on the floor

ought to use pit toilets"

— — — —

Granite creek Guard station   9 July

   the boulder in the creek never moves
       the water is always falling
     together!

A ramshackle little cabin built by Frank Beebe the miner.
Two days walk to here from roadhead.
       arts of the Japanese: moon-watching
                  insect-hearing
Reading the sutra of Hui Nêng.

  one does not need universities and libraries
  one need be alive to what is about

saying "I don't care"

— — — —

11 July

cut fresh rhubarb by the bank
the creek is going down

2

last night caught a trout
today climbed to the summit of Crater Mountain and back
high and barren: flowers I don't recognize
ptarmigan and chicks, feigning the broken wing.

> Baxter: "Men are funny, once I loved a girl
> so bad it hurt, but I drove her away. She was
> throwing herself at me—and four months later she
> married another fellow."

A doe in the trail, unafraid.
A strange man walking south
A boy from Marblemount with buckteeth, learning machine shop.

- - - -

Crater Mountain   Elevation: 8049 feet   23 July

Really wretched weather for three days now—wind, hail, sleet,
snow; the FM transmitter is broken / rather the receiver is /
what can be done?

> Even here, cold foggy rocky place, there's life—4 ptarmigan
> by the A-frame, cony by the trail to the snowbank.

> hit my head on the lamp,
> the shutters fall, the radio quits,
> the kerosene stove won't stop, the wood stove
> won't start, my fingers are too numb to write.

& this is mid-July. At least I have energy enough to read
science-fiction. One has to go to bed fully clothed.

- - - -

The stove burning wet wood—windows misted over giving the blank white light of shoji. Outside wind blows, no visibility. I'm filthy with no prospect of cleaning up. (Must learn yoga-system of Patanjali—)

— — — —

Crater Shan   28 July

Down for a new radio, to Ross Lake, and back up. Three days walking. Strange how unmoved this place leaves one; neither articulate or worshipful; rather the pressing need to look within and adjust the mechanism of perception.

A dead sharp-shinned hawk, blown by the wind against the lookout. Fierce compact little bird with a square head.

—If one wished to write poetry of nature, where an audience? Must come from the very conflict of an attempt to articulate the vision   poetry & nature in our time.

                    (reject the human; but the tension of
                    human events, brutal and tragic, against
                    a non-human background? like Jeffers?)

— — — —

Pair of eagles soaring over Devil's Creek canyon

— — — —

31 July

This morning:
                    floating face down in the water bucket
            a drowned mouse.

4

*"Were it not for Kuan Chung, we should be wearing our hair
unbound and our clothes buttoning on the left side"*

> A man should stir himself with poetry
> Stand firm in ritual
> Complete himself in music
> > > lun yü

————

Comparing the panoramic Lookout View photo dated 8 August
1935: with the present view. Same snowpatches; same shapes.
Year after year; snow piling up and melting.

> "By God" quod he, "for pleynly, at a word
> Thy drasty ryming is not worth a tord."

————

Crater Shan   3 August

How pleasant to squat in the sun
Jockstrap & zoris

form—leaving things out at the right spot
ellipse, is emptiness
> > > these ice-scoured valleys
> > > swarming with plants
> "I am the Queen Bee!
> > > Follow Me!"

————

Or having a wife and baby,
    living close to the ocean, with skills for
    gathering food.

5

QUEBEC DELTA 04 BLACK

Higgins to Pugh (over)
 "the wind comes out of the east
  or northeast,
  the chimney smokes all over the room.
  the wind comes out of the west;
  the fire burns clean."

Higgins L.O. reads the news:
 "flying saucer with a revolving black band
  drouth in the south.
Are other worlds watching us?"
The rock alive, not barren.
  flowers lichen pinus albicaulis chipmunks
mice even grass.

—first I turn on the radio
—then make tea & eat breakfast
—study Chinese until eleven

—make lunch, go chop snow to melt for water,
read Chaucer in the early afternoon.

  "Is this real
   Is this real
   This life I am living?"
     —Tlingit or Haida song

      — — — —

"Hidden Lake to Sourdough"
—"This is Sourdough"
—"Whatcha doing over there?"
—"Readin some old magazines
   they had over here."

      — — — —

6

6 August

Clouds above and below, but I can see Kulshan, Mt. Terror,
Shuksan; they blow over the ridge between here and
Three-fingered Jack, fill up the valleys. The Buckner Boston
Peak ridge is clear.

What happens all winter; the wind driving snow; clouds—
wind, and mountains—repeating

this is what always happens here,

and the photograph of a young female torso hung in the lookout
window, in the foreground. Natural against natural, beauty.

two butterflies
a chilly clump of mountain
flowers.

zazen   non-life.   An art: mountain-watching.

leaning in the doorway whistling
a chipmunk popped out
listening

— — — —

9 August

Sourdough: Jack, do you know if a fly is an electrical
    conductor? (over)
Desolation: A fly? Are you still trying to electrocute flies? (over)
Sourdough: Yeah   I can make em twitch a little. I got five
    number six batteries on it (over)
Desolation: I don't know, Shubert, keep trying. Desolation
    clear.

— — — —

7

10 August

First wrote a haiku and painted a haiga for it; then repaired
the Om Mani Padme Hum prayer flag, then constructed a stone
platform, then shaved down a shake and painted a zenga on it,
then studied the lesson.

> a butterfly
> scared up from its flower
> caught by the wind and swept over the cliffs
> SCREE

Vaux Swifts: in great numbers, flying before the storm,
arcing so close that the sharp wing-whistle is heard.

> "The śrāvaka
disciplined in Tao, enlightened, but on the wrong path."
summer,
> on the west slopes creek beds are brushy
> north-faces of ridges, steep and
> covered late with snow

> slides and old burns on dry hills.

(In San Francisco: I live on the Montgomery Street drainage
—at the top of a long scree slope just below a cliff.)

— — — —

sitting in the sun in the doorway
picking my teeth with a broomstraw
listenin to the buzz of the flies.

— — — —

12 August

        A visit all day, to the sheep camp, across the
glacier and into Devil's park. A tent under a clump of Alpine
fir; horses, sheep in the meadow.

              take up solitary occupations.

Horses stand patiently, rump to the wind.
           —gave me one of his last two cigars.

Designs, under the shut lids, glowing in sun

        (experience! that drug.)
Then the poor lonely lookouts, radioing forth and back.

After a long day's travel, reached the ridge,
followed a deer trail down
              to five small lakes.
in this yuga, the moral imperative is to COMMUNICATE.
Making tea.

fewer the artifacts, less the words,
            slowly the life of it
a knack for non-attachment.

Sourdough radioing to the smoke-chaser crew

"you're practically there
you gotta go up the cliff
you gotta cross the rock slide
look for a big blaze on a big tree
        [two climbers killed by lightning
          on Mt. Stuart]
"are you on the timber stand
or are you on the side of the cliff?

Say, Bluebell, where are you?
A patch of salmonberry and tag-alder to the right"
        —must take a look.

————

Cratershan   15 August

When the mind is exhausted of images, it invents its own.

      orange juice is what she asked for
         bright chrome restaurant, 2 a.m.
      the rest of us drinking coffee
      but the man brought orange pop.   haw!

late at night, the eyes tired, the teapot empty, the tobacco damp.

Almost had it last night: *no identity*. One thinks, "I emerged
from some general, non-differentiated thing, I return to it." One
has in reality never left it; there is no return.
                      my language fades.   Images of erosion.

"That which includes all change never changes; without change
time is meaningless; without time, space is destroyed. Thus we
arrive at the void."

————

"If a Bodhisattva retains the thought of an ego, a person, a
being, or a soul, he is no more a Bodhisattva."

      You be Bosatsu,
      I'll be the taxi-driver
      Driving you home.

10

The curious multi-stratified metamorphic rock. Blue and white, clouds reaching out. To survive a winter here learn to browse and live in holes in the rocks under snow.

Sabi: One does not have a great deal to give. That which one does give has been polished and perfected into a spontaneous emptiness; sterility made creative, it has no pretensions, and encompasses everything.

Zen view, o.k.?

– – – –

21 August

Oiling and stowing the tools. (artifact / tools: now there's a topic.)
When a storm blows in, covering the south wall with rain and blotting out the mountains. Ridges look new in every light. Still discovering new conformations——every cony has an ancestry but the rocks were just here.

Structure in the lithosphere / cycles of change in rock / only the smallest percentage sanded and powdered and mixed with life-derived elements.
Is chemical reaction a type of perception??—Running through all things   motion and reacting, object against object / there is more than enough time for all things to happen: swallowing its own tail.

– – – –

Diablo Dam   24 August

Back down off Crater in a snowstorm, after closing up the lookout. With Baxter from Granite Creek all the way to the

dam for more supplies. Clouds on the rocks; rain falls and
falls. Tomorrow we shall fill the packs with food and return to
Granite Creek.

———

In San Francisco: September 13.

Boys on bicycles in the asphalt playground wheeling and circling
aimlessly like playful gulls or swallows. Smell of a fresh-parked
car.

———

B. Sourdough

Marblemount Ranger Station   27 June 53

The antique car managed it to Marblemount last week, and then
to Koma Kulshan for a week of gnats, rain, & noise.
    The Philosophy of the Forest Service: Optimistic view of
nature—democratic, utilitarian. "Nature is rational." Equals,
treat it right and it will make a billion board feet a year. Paradox
suppressed. What wd an Aristocratic F.S. be like? Man traps?

Forest equals crop / Scenery equals recreation / Public equals
money.   : : The shopkeeper's view of nature.

> Hail Mr. Pulaski, after whom the Pulaski
> Tool is named.

—the iron stove, the windows, and the trees. "It is, and is not, I
am sane enough." Get so you don't have to think about what
you're doing because you *know* what you're doing.

12

J. Francis: Should I marry? It would mean a house; and the next thirty years teaching school." LOOKOUT!

Old McGuire and the fire of 1926: 40,000 acres on the upper Skagit, a three-mile swathe. Going to scrub my clothes & go down to Sedro-Woolley now with Jack.

— — — —

28 June

A day off—went to Bellingham and out to Gooseberry Bay, the Lummi reservation. Past a shed with three long cedar canoes in it. Finally to where the Lummi Island ferry stops, and this was about the end of the road, but we could drive a little farther on, and it was there we went through the Kitchen Midden. Through it, because the road cut right through shells and oysters and all. While looking at this a lady in a house shouted out to us; then came closer, & said if you're interested in the kitchen midden "as such" come out in back and "look where we had it bulldozed." And I said how do you like living on somebody's old kitchen heap, and she said it made her feel kind of funny sometimes. Then I said, well it's got about 3000 years in it vertical, but that might be dead wrong. It was 10 feet high, 45 feet wide, and 325 feet long, with one cedar stump on it about 110 years old, to show when (at least) it was finished with. Full of oyster, butter clam, cockle, mussel, snail and assorted shells.

We went back by the same road and at the outskirts of Bellingham Jack pointed out a ratty looking place called Coconut Grove where he said he had spent time drinking with a "rough crowd." They drank beer out of steins and called the place the Cat's Eye instead.

Outskirts of Bellingham, something of clear sky to the west over the waters of Puget Sound, the San Juan islands; and very black clouds up the Skagit, toward the vast mountain wilderness of the North Cascades. We turned off 99 to go into that black, wet hole, and it did start raining pretty quick after we went up that road. Coffee in Sedro-Woolley, a sign "No Drinks Served to Indians" and there are many Indians, being strawberry picking season, and Loggerodeo is next week. Marblemount Ranger Station about 8.30 & in the bunkhouse found a magazine with an article about an eighteen-year-old girl who could dance and paint and compose and sew and was good looking, too, with lots of pictures.

– – – –

Story: a Tarheel at Darrington had this nice dog. One day he was out dynamiting fish—threw a stick of powder into the water, all lit and ready to go. The dog jumped in, retrieved it, and ran back with it in his mouth. The logger took off up a tree shouting —Git back, Dog! Then it blasted. Tarheel still limps.
—Blackie.

—And then there was this young married couple, who stay locked in their room four weeks—when friends finally break in all they find is two assholes, jumping back and forth through each other.   " " "

– – – –

Ruby Creek Guard Station   30 June

The foamy wake behind the boat *does* look like the water of Hokusai. Water in motion is precise and sharp, clearly formed, holding specific postures for infinitely small frozen moments.
    Four mules: Tex, Barney Oldfield, Myrtle, Bluejay.
Four horses: Willy, Skeezix, Blaze, Mabel.

– – – –

14

Sourdough Mountain Lookout   Elevation: 5977 feet
17 July 53

"GREENEST Goddam kid I EVER saw. Told him he couldn't
boil beans at that altitude, he'd have to fry them. When I left I
said, now, be careful, this is something you gotta watch out
about, don't flog your dummy too much! And he says real
serious, Oh no, I won't. Hawww—"
"And then he was trying to fry an egg and he missed the pan
and he missed the stove and landed the egg on both feet, he
didn't know whether to run, shit, or go blind!"

Just managed to get through to Phil Whalen, on the radio, him
up on Sauk Lookout now.

Rode up here on Willy the Paint, a pleasant white-eyed little
horse that took great caution on rock and snow. Had to lead him
across the whitewater at Sourdough Creek. Horses look noble
from the side, but they sure are silly creatures when seen from
the front. Mules just naturally silly—Whenever we stopped,
Myrtle would commence kicking Bluejay & Bluejay would kick
Barney, all with great WHACKS on the forkies, but Tex
behaved, being neither kicked nor kicking. Shoeing Willy
required the twitch, anvil, nails, three of us, and great sweating
groaning and swearing. Blackie whacks him with a hammer
while Roy twists his nose to make him be good.
    This is the place to observe clouds and the gradual dissolution
of snow. Chipmunk got himself locked in here and when I tried
to shoo him out he'd just duck in a corner. Finally when I was
sorting screws he came out and climbed up on the waterbucket
looking I guess for a drink—hung on, face down, with his hind
legs only to the edge of the pail, inside, for a long time, and
finally fell in. Helped him out, splashing about—nobody been
there he'd have drunned.
    Keep looking across to Crater Mountain and get the funny
feeling I am up there looking out, right now, "because there are

no calendars in the mountains" —shifting of light & cloud,
perfection of chaos, magnificent *jiji mu-ge* / interlacing
interaction.

— — — —

Sourdough Mountain Lookout   19 July

Up at a quarter to six, wind still blowing the mist through the
trees and over the snow. Rins'd my face in the waterhole at the
edge of the snowfield—ringed with white rock and around that,
heather. Put up the SX aerial on a long pole made by some
lookout of years past, sticks & limbs & trunks all wired and tied
together. Made a shelf for papers out of half an old orange crate,
and turned the radio receiver off. Walked down the ridge, over
the snow that follows so evenly the very crest—snow on the
north slope, meadows and trees on the south. Small ponds, lying
in meadows just off the big snowfields, snags, clumps of
mountain hemlock, Alpine fir, a small amount of Alaska cedar.
   Got back, built a fire and took the weather. About six, two
bucks came, one three-point, one four-point, very warily, to
nibble at huckleberries and oats and to eat the scraps of mouldy
bacon I threw out. Shaggy and slender, right in the stiff wind
blowing mist over the edge of the ridge, or out onto the
snowfield, standing out clear and dark against the white. Clouds
keep shifting—totally closed in; a moment later across to
Pyramid Peak or up Thunder Creek it's clear. But the wind
stays.
   Now I've eaten dinner and stuffed the stove with twisted
pitchy Alpine fir limbs. Clumps of trees fading into a darker and
darker gray. White quartz veins on the rocks out the south
window look like a sprinkling of snow. Cones on the top boughs
of the Alpine fir at the foot of the rocks a DARK PURPLE,
stand perfectly erect, aromatic clusters of LINGAMS fleshy and
hard.

16

Lookout free talk time on the radio band: Saul called Koma Kulshan, Church called Sauk, Higgins is talking to Miner's Ridge. Time to light the lamp.

– – – –

23 July

Days mostly cloudy—clouds breaking up to let peaks through once in a while. Logan, Buckner, Boston, Sahale, Snowpeak, Pyramid, Névé, Despair, Terror, Fury, Challenger. And the more distant Redoubt and Glacier Peak. As well as Hozomeen and Three Fingered Jack. Right now looking down on the Skagit—pink clouds—pale rose-water pink, with soft shadings of gray and lavender, other combinations of pastel reds and blues, hanging over Pyramid Peak.

Fretting with the Huang Po doctrine of Universal Mind. What a thorny one.

– – – –

25 July

Last night: thunderstorm. A soft piling of cumulus over the Little Beaver in late afternoon—a gradual thickening and darkening. A brief shower of hail that passed over & went up Thunder Creek valley: long gray shreds of it slowly falling and bent in the wind—while directly above Ruby Creek sunlight is streaming through. Velvety navy blue over Hozomeen, with the sun going down behind Mt. Terror and brilliant reds and pinks on the under-clouds, another red streak behind black Hozomeen framed in dark clouds. Lightning moving from Hozomeen slowly west into red clouds turning gray, then black; rising wind. Sheet lightning pacing over Little Beaver, fork lightning striking Beaver Pass.

This morning a sudden heavy shower of rain and a thick fog. A buck scared: ran off with stiff springy jumps down the snowfield. Throwing sprays of snow with every leap: head held stiffly high.

– – – –

9 August

Sourdough radio relay to Burns:

to: Ray Patterson, District Assistant, Early Winters
     Ranger Station.
from: Jud Longmoor.
     "Kit, Ted and Lucky went out over Deception Pass
     probably headed for airport. Belled but not
     hobbled. Horse took out in night, August 3, above
     Fish Camp. The Shull Creek trail is not passable now.
     Mt. Baker string will pack us to Skypilot Pass
     Thursday August 5. Have Ken Thompson meet us there
     with pack string and saddle horse for Loring. We
     will have pack gear and riding saddle."

Lightning storm again: first in twilight the long jagged ones back of Terror & Fury, later moving down Thunder Creek, and then two fires: right after the strikes, red blooms in the night. Clouds drifting in & obscuring them.

– – – –

Discipline of self-restraint is an easy one; being clear-cut, negative, and usually based on some accepted cultural values.

Discipline of following desires, *always* doing what you want to
do, is hardest. It presupposes self-knowledge of motives,
a careful balance of free action and sense of where the cultural
taboos lay—knowing whether a particular "desire" is instinctive,
cultural, personal, a product of thought, contemplation,
or the unconscious. Blake: if the doors of perception were
cleansed, everything would appear to man as it is, infinite. For
man has closed himself up, 'til all he sees is through narrow
chinks of his caverns. Ah.

> the frustrate bumblebee turns over
> clambers the flower's center upside down
> furious hidden buzzing
> near the cold sweet stem.

In a culture where the aesthetic experience is denied
and atrophied, genuine religious ecstasy rare, intellectual
pleasure scorned—it is only natural that sex should become
the only personal epiphany of most people & the culture's
interest in romantic love take on staggering size.

The usefulness of hair on the legs: mosquitoes and
deerflies have to agitate it in drawing nigh the
skin—by that time warned—Death to Bugs.

(an empty water glass is no less empty than a universe
full of nothing) —the desk is under the pencil.

— — — —

Sourdough Mountain Lookout   12 August

3:55 p.m.   Desolation calls in his weather.
4:00   Sourdough starts calling Marblemount.
4:00   Sam Barker asks for the air: "Dolly,

19

call the doctor at Concrete and have him
go up to Rockport.   There's a man got hurt
up here."

4:01   Marblemount: "Up where?"
4:01   Barker: "Up here on Sky Creek. A fellow from
              Stoddard's logging outfit."
4:01   Marblemount: "Okay Sam. Marblemount clear."
4:10   Sourdough calls his weather in to Marblemount.
4:11   Barker: "Dolly, did you make that call through?"
4:11   Marblemount: "You mean for the doctor?"
4:12   Barker: "Yeah. Well the man's dead."
4:12   Marblemount: "Who was he?"
4:12   Barker: "I don't know, the one they call the
              Preacher."
4:13   Somebody I couldn't hear, calling Marblemount.
4:13   Marblemount: "The Sky Creek trail. I don't know.
              Somebody they call the Preacher." Marblemount
              clear.

- - - -

14 August

   11.30 Hidden Lake spots a smoke; he hardly gets an azimuth
in to Marblemount but I've got it too & send my reading in.
Then all the other Lookouts in the North Cascades catch it—
a big column in the Baker River District, between Noisy
and Hidden Creeks.
   So Phil on Sauk Mountain is busy calling Darrington and
Marblemount for the suppression crews, and then the patrol plane
comes to look at it and says it's about six acres of alpine
timber. & the trucks are off, and Willey the cook has to go too,
and the plane flies over to drop supplies at a fire-fighter's camp.

- - - -

20

Don't be a mountaineer, be a mountain.
            And shrug off a few with avalanches.

Sourdough Mountain at the hub of six valleys: Skagit,
Thunder, Ruby, Upper Skagit, Pierce Creek, Stetattle creek.

- - - -

20 August

  Skirt blown against her hips, thighs, knees
                hair over her ears
        climbing the steep hill in high-heeled shoes

(the Deer come for salt, not affection)

—Government Confucianism, as in the *Hsiao-ching* / Filial
Piety—a devilish sort of liberalism. Allowing you should
give enough justice and food to prevent a revolution, yet surely
keeping the people under the thumb. "If you keep the taxes
just low enough, the people will not revolt, and you'll get rich."
Movements against this psychology—the Legalistic rule of
Ch'in; Wang An-shih perhaps?
                This is Chinese; plus Blake's collected,
Walden and sumi painting, pass the time.

- - - -

  Nature a vast set of conventions, totally arbitrary, patterns
and stresses that come into being each instant; could disappear
totally anytime; and continues only as a form of play: the
cosmic / comic   delight.
                "For in this period the Poet's work is done
and all the great events of time start forth and are conceived in

such a period, within a moment, a Pulsation of the artery."
        —True insight a love-making hovering
between the void & the immense worlds of creation. To
symbolically represent Prajña as female is right. The
Prajña girl statue from Java.

– – – –

22 August

Old Roy Raymond hike up and see me. About noon I'm
chopping wood. We spend the afternoon playing horseshoes with
mule-shoes; this morning playing poker.
    "My Missus died a few years ago so I sold the house
    and the furniture 'til I got it down now to where I can get
    everything into a footlocker. My friends'd ask me
    What you sell that for, & hell, what use did I have for it?
    I'll never marry again."
So he spends his time in the mountains—construction
jobs, forestry, mining. Winters in Aberdeen.
    Kim on Desolation radios over (evenings) to read bits of
picturesque speech and patter from antique *Reader's Digests* he's
found chez Lookout.

– – – –

Ross Lake Guard Station   31 August

Friday morning with snow coming in and storms all
across the North Cascades, straight down from Canada,
Blackie radios to come down. Work all morning with
inventory; put the shutters down & had to pack an enormous
load of crap off the mountain. About 85 pounds.
    Forest Service float on Ross Lake: all on a big raft;
corrugated walls and roofing. Porch with woodpile. A floating

dock with crosscuts, falling saws, spikes, wood, in't. At one end
the green landing barge moored alongside. The main raft, with
a boat-size wood door; inside a tangle of tools, beds, groceries.
A vast Diesel marine engine-block in the middle of the deck with
a chainsaw beside it. Kim on a cot next to that. Shelves on the
unpainted wall with rice, coffee, pancake syrup. Cords, vices,
wires on the workbench. A screen cooler full of bacon and ham.
And this enters, under the same roof, into another dock-room in
which the patrol boat floats, full of green light from the water.
Around the edge bales of hay and drums of Diesel. Moored
alongside outside, the horse raft. Covered with straw and
manure. A sunny windy day, lapping the logs.

– – – –

Trail crew work up Big Beaver Creek   4 September

    Crosscutting a very large down cedar across the trail and
then wedging, Kim gets below Andy bellers out
"Get your goddamn ass out of there you fuckin squarehead
you wanna get killed?"
    We make an extra big pot of chocolate pudding at
the shelter that night, make Kim feel better.

    Surge Milkers: "This man had a good little brown
heifer that gave lots of milk, and one morning he put the
milker on her and went back inside and fell asleep
and slept an hour. And that little heifer had
mastitis in two days."

– – – –

Hitching south   ca. 21 Sept

    Down from Skykomish, evening light,
back of a convertible wind whipping the blanket

clear sky darkening, the road winding along the river
willow and alder on the bank, a flat stretch of
green field; fir-covered hills beyond, dark
new barns and old barns—silvery shake barns—
          the new barns with tall round roofs.

                    — — — —

In Berkeley: 1 October 53

        "I am here to handle some of the preliminary
                    arrangements for the Apocalypse.
          Sand in pockets, sand in hair,
          Cigarettes that fell in seawater
          Set out to dry in the sun.
          Swimming in out of the way places
          In very cold water, creek or surf
          Is a great pleasure."
Under the Canary Island Pine
zazen and eating lunch.   We are all immortals
                    & the ground is damp.

24

REVIEW

Indian Legends of the Pacific Northwest. Ella E. Clark.
(Berkeley and Los Angeles: University of California Press,
1953.) Illustrated by Robert Bruce Inverarity.

Miss Clark forearms herself against the cavils of specialists
by announcing, in her introduction, an approach never
"sociological or anthropological." She has assembled over
a hundred tales from Oregon and Washington tribes;
one quarter from ethnological collections, one quarter from
informants, and half from writings and MSS of early
missionaries, travelers, army officers, etc. The book
is admittedly not representative of the whole range of
Pacific Northwest oral literature: ". . . my chief purpose
has been to prepare a collection of Pacific Northwest
myths and legends that the general reader will
enjoy, either as entertainment or as information about
an American way of living strange to him." The result is a
book almost entirely oriented around topography and
natural phenomena, and consisting for the most part of short local
legends and explanatory tales. The remaining selections are
Coyote-Transformer myths, a few dangerous-being tales,
two versions of the Star-Husband, and other inoffensive tales.
Indian Legends is organized in five sections: "Myths of
the Mountains"; "Legends of the Lakes"; "Tales of
the Rivers, Rocks and Waterfalls"; "Myths of Creation,
the Sky and Storms"; and "Miscellaneous Myths
and Legends." The contributing tribes are almost equally
divided between Interior and Coast groups, the

Yakima leading with eight tales, and the Quileute represented by seven. The rest—thirty-six tribes—average two or three tales apiece. There are fifteen tales in the book for which no tribe is listed, and five specified as "various tribes." The book is provided with a bibliography, glossary, and source notes.

Given her five categories, and the fact that this collection is made along geographical rather than cultural lines, Miss Clark has succeeded in creating a surprisingly well-integrated book. By means of headnotes and introductory passages to the five sections, she establishes the basic unity of Raven, Coyote, Kwatee and Bluejay as "Changers," and manages to minimize the cultural differences between Coast and Plateau tribes. She has rewritten most of the tales, imparting a unity of style to the collection. Miss Clark tends to enlarge some on the original sources, and (as in her version of the Snohomish tale, "Why Rivers Flow but One Way") inserting material not in the listed source to give the various tales more cohesion. One gets the feeling, especially in the first half of the book, that "The Great Spirit" appears too frequently —but this can probably be accounted for by the fact that her local legends are largely derived from earlier, non-anthropological sources that romanticized Indian folklore. Although there may be some danger in exposing the general reader to such a quantity of questionable source material, perhaps the greatest value of this book for the folklorist is that it does bring together a variety of minor tales from neglected and obscure sources, providing a basis for comparison with the standard ethnological collections.

Just how much the general reader will actually enjoy this book is another question. I cannot believe that even natives of the Pacific Northwest would prefer dozens of small anecdotes about local mountains and lakes to a few of the highly imaginative supernatural—and animal-marriage tales of the type Miss Clark has entirely omitted. Furthermore, the reader with some interest in literature cannot help but be confused when he discovers a Modoc myth on the supernatural origin of the Indians under "Mountains" because it mentions Mt. Shasta en passant, or a Klamath version of the Coyote monster-killing (by being swallowed) tale among "Tales of the Rivers, Rocks and Waterfalls" because this particular monster happens to live in the Columbia. For Miss Clark— an English teacher at Washington State College, and a person presumably scrupulous about matters of terminology in English literature—to title her first three sections entirely for alliterative effect, seems highly capricious.

One cannot expect, granted the present attitude of the Postal Authorities, that the best of Pacific Northwest oral literature, with its Rabelaisian-Dadaist overtones, could be presented to the general public. But we should look forward to the time when an anthology of Northwest Coast literature, organized along culture-area rather than geographical lines, and making some attempt to separate genres and delineate styles, will be made available to intelligent readers: one containing the full wit, bite and dash of the original versions. Radin's *Winnebago Hero Cycles,* Boas' *Tsimshian Mythology,* Reichard's *Analysis of Coeur d'Alene Myths,* and Dell Skeels' excellent unpublished dissertation on Nez Percé oral literature (University of Washington) are all usable groundwork for such a book. It is a shame Miss Clark did not make some application of them.

Fall '54

Indian Tales. Jaime de Angulo. Foreword by Carl Carmer. (New York: A. A. Wyn, 1953.)

American Indian folktales are available in large numbers to a small public in careful and scholarly translations. A great many of them are charming in this form, capturing unawares even those students bent on ethnographic data or in search of some worldwide motif. One rarely loses the sense, however, that these tales are translations, in writing. Jaime de Angulo has done a book that is not ethnography and not, strictly speaking, folktale translation, but is thoroughly Indian and a real tale told, not written.

The framework is the journey of Bear, his wife Antelope, and children Fox Boy and baby Quail through what can be identified as Northern California. In the course of this relatively realistic journey of half-human, half-animal figures, in a party that grows gradually larger through the addition of friends and relatives, eight stories are told.

Indian Tales was not intended to be read literally or as document: "I wrote these stories several years ago, for my children, when they were little. Some of them I invented out of my own head. Some of them I remembered—at least, parts, which I wove in and out. Some parts I actually translated almost word for word. I have mixed tribes that don't belong together . . . So don't worry about it." It seems ungracious to go ahead and worry about it, but those who come to *Indian Tales* with a baggage of knowledge and interest in California folklore are not going to be able to help themselves. What they will find, roughly, is a story that might be told by Indians of a real journey through objective territory by real people, after the telling of it had been filtered through several generations and the real people become confused with the half-animals of folklore.

References to *Khalimatoto* (Thunderer) in the Kuksu ceremony make it possible to identify the Bear family with Pomo. Their home can be located near Clear Lake. They all set out on a trip to visit the sister of Antelope, who has married into the Crane people, and travel through the areas of Hawk people, Flint people, Grass, Fire and Water people— who cannot be identified with anything. Bear's family is joined, en route, by Grandfather Coyote, Grizzly Bear and his daughter, and a party of Antelope people. They arrive at the land

of the Cranes, who are clearly Yurok, and later Karok, and
go to Katimin, a real Karok village on the Klamath River,
where they watch the White Deerskin Dance and World-renewal
Ceremony. Antelope is disappointed with her sister, who has
". . . changed too much; she was always talking about
insults and payment for insults and money and valuable things."
After this entirely credible touch, the party goes northwest,
around Mt. Shasta, to what can be considered Grass Lake, where
the Antelope leave to go to their home over the mountains.
Then they cut south down the Adzumma (Pit) River to
the village of Dalmooma, which is occupied by Wolves.
(Dalmooma was an Achomawi village.) At Dalmooma they
watch a fight between Wolves and Wildcats (Modoc) and
then, with a Wolf boy, travel home, across the Sacramento
valley and into the Coast range. Back in Bear territory,
Fox Boy goes through the Kuksu initiation. After an easy
winter, the party starts out north again, but before they reach
Crane country, belief becomes unsuspended: Fox Boy begins (as
a result of his initiation?) to become more "human," Kilelli
(a new addition) successfully wins a "power" and Fox Boy
and his friend Oriole Girl stop the story by refusing to
believe in the teller, Mr. de Angulo.

A variety of details show that de Angulo truly did mix
the tribes up, but in the friendly arguments of "Crane"
shamanism versus "Wolf" methods of curing, and other minor
issues, a good deal of anthropological fact leaks through.
The eight stories told in the course of marching add to texture
and confusion. There are two creation myths: one told by
Grandfather Coyote about his ancestor (or himself, it is
never clear) as culture hero; the other by a Wolf person in
which Coyote figures as Tricksters, and Silver Fox (an
Achomawi figure) is creator. The other stories include typical
North California material, but in such mixtures as to make
a search for origins unprofitable, as well as unimaginative. One
has the feeling that it is totally authentic.

Stylistically, the use of capitalization, repetition and imitative

sound (sound of travelling: *tras . . . tras . . . tras . . .*)
gives the narrative its "spoken" effect, and a deceptive
simplicity. At some points the language falls down, as when
Bear got to his feet "ponderously, as befitted an old man"—
showing a "literary" tendency that becomes strong toward the
end of the book. Embedded in the text are a number of
poems or "songs." The ten pages of Coyote Old Man's "Shaman
Songs" contain some small poems that have a sharpness
and compression approaching haiku.

Perhaps the most important, and surely the most enigmatic
character in the book is Coyote Old Man. He is awakened
from an ageless sleep by the Bear party:

> Old Coyote was sleeping in the hills.
> Old Coyote was sleeping in his house.
> His house was back in the back of the hills
> In a little valley, in a hidden valley away back in the hills.

Although he joins Bear and his friends, he says little and only
tells two stories. When questioned—is he the very same
Coyote he tells about? And, what is the difference between
animal-people and real-people? He answers, ". . . I am
Coyote Old Man. I am a very old man. I am a thousand years
old. *I know what happened after the before* and before
the after!" His real identity, in this completely delightful book,
is the culture-hero who listened patiently to gossip,
could sit still, eat acorn-mush with the rest, and remember
for years: Jaime de Angulo.

Spring '54

JAPAN FIRST TIME
AROUND

"Arita Maru"   at sea   7: V: 56

Red ooze of the North Pacific—only sharks' teeth and the
earbones of whales. An endless mist of skeletons, settling
to the ocean floor.
Marine limestone in the Himalaya at 20,000 feet
breadfruit, laurel, cinnamon and figtree grew in Greenland—
cretaceous. "Length of fetch" the distance a batch of waves
has run without obstruction.
salts—diatoms—copepods—herring—fishermen—us. eating.

A sudden picture of Warm Springs Camp A loggers making
flower arrangements in the yellow-pine tokonomas of their
plank camp cabins. I'd work hard all day for that.
                  any single thing or complex of things
literally as great as the whole.
            wild lilac and lizards / blowing seafog down the hill.
A square is: because the world is round.

At sea   16: V: 56

Moon in the first quarter sinking a path of light on the sea;
Jupiter by the sickle of Leo in the west, Cygnus and Lyra

in the east, Delphinus just over the haze of the night horizon.
The tail of Scorpio in the water.

           POETRY is to give access to persons—
cutting away the fear and reserve and camping of social life: thus
for Chinese poetry. Nature poetry too: "this is what I've
seen." Playing with the tools—language, myth, symbolism,
intellect—fair enough but childish to abuse.

    just where am I in this food-chain?

– – – –

    Red-tailed Tropic birds, and fields of plankton. Lawrence,
in *Aaron's Rod:* "The American races—and the South
Sea islanders—the Marquesans, the Maori blood. That was the
true blood. It wasn't frightened."
 . . . "Why don't you be more like the Japanese you talk
about? Quiet, aloof little devils. They don't bother about being
loved. They keep themselves taut in their own selves—
there, at the bottom of the spine, the devil's own power they've
got there."

           Lawrence and his fantastic, accurate, lopsided
intuitions. The American Indians and Polynesians developed great
cultures and almost deliberately kept their populations
down.   and again,

    "Love is a process of the incomprehensible human soul:
love also incomprehensible but still only a process. The
process should work to a completion, not to some horror of
intensification and extremity wherein the soul and body
ultimately perish. The completion of the process of love is the
arrival at a state of simple, pure self-possession, for man
and woman. Only that."

– – – –

At sea   21: V   and into Kobe

Coasting along Wakayama: the sharp cut steep green haze
hills, boats about, high-prowed dip slop in wave wash and new
white-bellied birds following wave-lick over, then, morning
passing—sitting under a lifeboat watching land slip by.
Beyond Awaji Isle—jokes about Genji. Into the long smoggy
Osaka Bay leading finally up to Kobe—ship upon ship—
rusty Korean tiny freighters—and to the pier.
A truckload of Seals on the road by Customs snaking their
small heads about. And train, and thousands of crowded
tile-roof houses along the track, patches of tended ground;
O man—poorness and small houses.

— — — —

Kyoto   23: V: 56

. . . some Americans here make reference to short hours of
sleep and simple food—good Xrist you'd think Zen was just a
roundabout way for the rich to live like the workingman—there
are friends in America who are humble about their interest in
the Dharma and ashamed of their profligacy while living on
salvaged vegetables and broken rice—sleep six hours a night so
as to study books and think, and so to work, to keep the wife
and kids: what foppery is this—and it turns out you got to
spend $30 for a special meditation cushion. The center in this
world is quietly moving to San Francisco where it's most
alive—these Japanese folks may be left behind and they won't
(in the words of Fêng Kuan) recognize it when they see it.

— — — —

25: V

Today up Hiei-zan. Jodo-in, young bonze named Somon; the
tomb of Dengyo Daishi. Vast cool wooden temple in the

mountain shade—it smells good. A monk in white came with
lunch on trays: pickles and rice and peas. Then W. and I
went to the main room and picture of Dengyo Daishi, and a
small shrine room to Kwannon that looked like a peyote dream.
(the only superstitions that are really
dangerous to peasant Buddhist types are the superstitions of
nationalism and the state)
Then: in fog-rain and frog-croak climbed up and along by a
Cryptomeria sawmill (they fall trees same method we do
judging by the butt cuts) to another temple; finally below
that an even larger temple recently repainted—went in and lit
candles. Uguisu don't sing, they shout.

– – – –

7: VI

. . . one begins to see the connecting truths hidden in Zen,
Avatamsaka and Tantra. The giving of a love relationship is a
Bodhisattva relaxation of personal fearful defenses and
self-interest strivings—which communicates unverbal to the
other and leaves *them* do the same. "Enlightenment" is
this interior ease and freedom carried not only to persons but to
all the universe, such-such-and void—which is in essence
and always, freely changing and interacting. The emptiness of
"both self and things"—only a Bodhisattva has no
Buddha-nature. (Lankavatara-sūtra.)
So, Zen being founded on Avatamsaka, and the net-network of
things; and Tantra being the application of the "interaction
with no obstacles" vision on a personal-human level—the
"other" becomes the lover, through whom the various links in
the net can be perceived. As Zen goes to *anything* direct—
rocks or bushes or people—the Zen Master's presence
is to help one keep attention undivided, to always look one
step farther along, to simplify the mind: like a blade
which sharpens to nothing.

34

Tantra, Avatamsaka and Zen really closely historically
related: and these aspects of philosophy and practice were done
all at once, years ago, up on Hiei-zan. Knit old
dharma-trails.

— — — —

An ant is dragging a near-dead fly through the mosswoods by
the tongue.

        —dreamed of a new industrial-age dark ages:
filthy narrow streets and dirty buildings with rickety walks over
the streets from building to building—unwashed illiterate
brutal cops—a motocycle cop and sidecar drove up and over
a fat workingman who got knocked down in a fight—
tin cans and garbage and drooping electric wires everywhere—

— — — —

15: VI

Leaving the temple this morning walked by a small fox shrine
where a Zen monk was chanting: there I heard the subtle
steady single-beat of oldest American-Asian shamanism. The
basic song. "Buddhist lectures on Shoshone texts" or
Shastra / commentaries on Navajo creation myth.

— — — —

Koen-ji   28: VI

Key to evolution adaptability: the organism alters itself
rather than continue fruitless competition.
                . . . logging camp morning, high clouds
moving east, birds, morning light on the pine and sugi;

everyone getting up to go to work. Chao-chou: "Wal I
been trainin horses for thirty yars and now I git kicked by a
dunkey."

—the brain and nervous system all infolded ectoderm:
thought but a kind of skin perception.

And now there are too many human beings. Let's be animals
or buddhas instead.

– – – –

The altar figure is Manjusri, in gold-lacquered wood. Not
only can you tell "enlightenment" from the face, but you can tell
how it was achieved. The old Zen Master statues in the
meditation hall show them as human beings who made it through
will, effort, years of struggle and intensity. Manjusri has the
face of a man who did it with cool intellect and comprehension,
cynicism and long historical views. Another made it by
poverty, wandering, and simple-minded self-sufficient
detachment.

Poking about in the abandoned monks' rooms—smell of an
old unused mining cabin or logging shanty—a cupboard of
bindles the boys left behind, a drawer full of letters, notebooks,
seals; like magazines and coffee cups full of dust and
mouseshit.

The old dark smoky kitchen where Han Shan might have worked.
Now making udon noodles out of wheat flour batter with a
pressing-and-cutting machine you crank by hand.

– – – –

Kyoto   30: IX

Nō play Yang Kuei Fei/Yōkihi——the episode of the
Shaman's visit to Hōrai (Jade nowhere Island place)—he
receives a hairpin, then she dances. The headdress gold-jewelled
triangles and floral danglers: quiver although the dancer

36

is immobile. A seismograph of imperceptible within. American
Nō stage: background painting a desert and distant
mountains? chorus on a long low bench. Maybe one large
real boulder.

———

Eternal crouching ancient women in dark smoky temple
kitchens, fanning the thornwood fire and dusting the hard black
dirt floor—once the virgin of what ritual? And gold glittering
temple hall?—
              self-discipline is bad for the character.
              THY HAND, GREAT ANARCH

"wisdom and berries grow on the same bush, but only one
could ever be plucked at one time" —Emerson's Journals (but
I knew a packer could chew copenhagen snoose while eating
huckleberries on opposite sides of the mouth and never did
mix em up). "The profoundly secret pass that leads from
fate to freedom."

———

6: X

   W. the tender secret sensitive square artist, all in himself,
a tiny smile, walks out and makes a clean bow, his head all
curly blond, and sits down at black piano, him in black. Against
the gold zigzag screen: and plays Haydn—as I could hear him
for weeks on, practicing in his corner of Rinko temple;
bluejeans and coffee in his double-sized-cup through hot days
and between naps. Decorous passionate music of Old Europe
out his Zen fingers, to the hall full of culture-thirsty student
boys and girls in blackwhite uniform, fierce-eyed and full of
orderly resentment, making their heart's Europe out of
thousandfold paperback translations, Aesop to Sartre—digging

this lush music. All in a land of rice paddy and green hills and rains where still deep-hatted Dharma-hobos try to roam.

– – – –

24: X

Leaves begin very gradually to fall—what crazy communion of the birds wheeling and circling back and forth in calling flock, above the pine and against sunset cold white-and-blue clouds—a bunch of birds being one——

Breaking the aspected realms into names—the "Three Realms" or the Trikaya or the "Three Worlds"—done a step farther, as mythology, and seeing the powers and aspects in terms of personalities and relationships archetypally expressed. As the three worlds are one, but seen as three from different angles, so the Goddess is mother, daughter, and wife at the same time. Indra's net is not merely two-dimensional. The movements of the triad of mother, father and child can be made to express any device of mythological or metaphysical thought.

(Beware of anything that promises freedom or enlightenment —traps for eager and clever fools—a dog has a keener nose— every creature in a cave can justify himself. Three-fourths of philosophy and literature is the talk of people trying to convince themselves that they really like the cage they were tricked into entering.)

> My love thoughts these days
> Come thick like the summer grass
> Which soon as cut and raked
> Grows wild again
>
> —Yakamochi

—two days contemplating ecology, food-chains and sex. Looking at girls as mothers or daughters or sisters for a change of view. Curious switch.

– – – –

13: XI

And dreamed that the Egyptian god Set appeared to me &
delivered a long prophetic poem, which I forgot.

O Muse who comes in a fiery cart wearing a skirt of revolving
swords, trumpeting and insistent; O Muse who comes through
the hedge wearing a gray coat, to stand under the ash-tree
beckoning . . .

Comes a time when the poet must choose: either to step
deep in the stream of his people, history, tradition, folding and
folding himself in wealth of persons and pasts; philosophy,
humanity, to become richly foundationed and great and sane
and ordered. Or, to step beyond the bound onto the way out,
into horrors and angels, possible madness or silly Faustian
doom, possible utter transcendence, possible enlightened return,
possible ignominious wormish perishing.

— — — —

22: XI   Founder's day at Daitoku-ji

A ringing bell starts it all—a few "cloud and water" monks
in traveling clothes, in a cluster, chatting under the pines at the
corner of the Dharma Hall. Colored banners. Priests in purple
and gold and Chinese high-toed slippers with raven-beak hats on.

A black-and-white dragon splashed across the ceiling glaring
down, body a circle in cloud and lightning—six burning
two-foot candles, and two four-foot pine boughs. Priests walk
in file scuffing the boat shoes. Sunshine comes in through
tree-beams; inside the hall here it's like a grove of Redwood, or
under a mountain. Oda Rōshi made eighteen bows.

— — — —

26: XI   Rinko-in

Barefoot down cold halls.

Maple red now glows, the high limbs first. Venus the morning
star—at daybreak and evening, sparrows hurtle in thousands.
Five men in jikatabi work-shoes slouching across the baseball
diamond by the Kamo river. A woman under the bridge
nursing her baby at noon hour, shovel and rake parked by.
Faint windy mists in the hills north—smoke and charcoal and
straw—at night hot soup "kasujiru" made of saké squeezings.
Little girls in long tan cotton stockings, red garters, still the
skimpy skirts. College boys cynically amble around in their
worn-flat geta clogs and shiny black uniforms looking raw, cold
and helpless. Big man on a motorcycle with a load of noodles.

"It is unspeakably wonderful to see a large volume of
water falling with a thunderous noise."

"Sparrows entertained me singing and dancing, I've
never had such a good time as today."

—Japanese lesson.

– – – –

21: I: 57   Daikan, period of Great Cold

Thick frost and a few flakes of dry cold snow; ice thick in the
stone hole water bowl boulder where the doves drink, frost
keen lines on all the twigs of the naked plum and each small
leaf of a tree.

EROTICISM of China and Japan a dark shadowy thing—a
perfumed cunt in a cave of brocades; Greek eroticism is
nakedness in full blast of sunlight; fucking on high sunny hills.
India is hips and breasts, agile limbs on stone floors with
intricate design.

Depth is the body. How does one perceive internal physical

40

states—yoga systems I guess—well well. soil conservation /
reforestation / birth control / spelling reform: "love the body."

- - - -

15: II: 57   Rinko-in

Fine clear morning sun melts frost—plum tree soon bloom—
Dove early to the stone water bowl (froze hard, so it walked
and pecked on it, no drink). Full moon last night—home from
zazen—flying eaves of the Dharma Hall silvery slate tile against
Orion—icy air slamming into the mouth. Stupid self dragging
its feet while I sit fooling with recall and fantasy—where the
sound or sight HITS and is transformed by the mental, at
THAT razoredge is the gate. MU is the wedge to chock it up
with, that very crack.

- - - -

12: III: 57   Tōdai-ji's "Water-gathering" ceremony

Tōdai-ji's enormous Chinese-Indian Gate of Power. Mangy
saw-horn bucks walking around. Mizutori, "water-gathering" at
Second Month temple. Grandaddy of all sugi trees in front.
Complex beaming and gabling—iron lanterns hanging, ornate,
faintly glowing. Far off dream lamps of former birth, exotic
and familiar. At seven p.m. monks run up the long stairway
with twenty-foot torches and wave and shake them at the
crowd, which delights to have the luck of standing under falling
clouds of sparks. Inside the hall, priests run clack-clack around
and around the central shrine in white wood shoes; stop, sit,
and blow conch-shells. They recite the names of all the Gods
of Japan, and all the thousands of Buddhas and Bodhisattvas.
It takes most of the night. Finally a group comes out and goes

down the steps to the well, makes two trips with decked-and-garlanded buckets of water to be blessed by Kwannon. Last, a bit more chanting and then the biggest torch of all is lit and danced INSIDE the hall by masked and head-dressed man—like a raven-beak—the bell bonging. Three a.m.

Later had breakfast with priests at a branch temple—came back on the early train to Kyoto watching the fresh snow-powdered hills and rising chill March sun, the last morning of the spring to wake up snowy. All those little houses, some smoking faint wispy blue in the long blue valley, and pure air.

— — — —

21: III

Kyoto City Hospital: Nurse girls in starch white scud through the halls in flocks—teal over the mountains—Nurse girls play ball in the yard, patients watching. In the next walled yard puppies on chains wait queer medical fates; a dead one belly up, strange tubes in his throat and intestines, beside two dull cowering dogs in filth.

— — — —

14: IV

Cherries, cherries—and over the hills from Pete's school—up past Hideyoshi's tomb and down and through a tunnel, out by a lake——on——air dry and dusty wind blowing—just rambling—drank saké on top of Higashiyama under a white petal-scattering tree. Down, almost trapped by the Miyako Hotel, on along the canal past drunk dancing grandmothers, and over brush hills, blue wild bushes blooming—again canal—to Pete's friend's house, a mycologist who does Nō and writes haiku and

paints—days gone thus, spring rambles and flowers; beyond
there lies——

————
/

9: V: 57

In the monastery sesshin / intensive meditation week: from
May Day on. One night I dreamt I was with Miura Rōshi, or
maybe an unheard of Polish revolutionary poet with a bald head
—looking at Berkeley. But a new Berkeley—of the future—
the Bay beach clean and white, the bay blue and pure; white
buildings and a lovely boulevard of tall Monterey pines that
stretched way back to the hills. We saw a girl from some ways
off walking toward us, long-legged, her hair bound loosely in
back.

SPRING SESSHIN AT SHOKOKU-JI

Shokoku Temple is in northern Kyoto, on level ground, with
a Christian college just south of it and many blocks of crowded
little houses and stone-edged dirt roads north. It is the mother-
temple of many branch temples scattered throughout Japan, and
one of the several great temple-systems of the Rinzai Sect of
Zen. Shokoku-ji is actually a compound: behind the big wood
gate and tile-topped crumbling old mud walls are a number of
temples each with its own gate and walls, gardens, and acres
of wild bamboo grove. In the center of the compound is the
soaring double-gabled Lecture Hall, silent and airy, an
enormous dragon painted on the high ceiling, his eye burning
down on the very center of the cut-slate floor. Except at
infrequent rituals the hall is unused, and the gold-gilt Buddha
sits on its high platform at the rear untroubled by drums and
chanting. In front of the Lecture Hall is a long grove of fine
young pines and a large square lotus-pond. To the east is a
wooden belltower and the unpretentious gate of the Sodo, the
training school for Zen monks, or Unsui.[1] They will become

[1] Unsui. The term is literally "cloud, water"—taken from a line of an
old Chinese poem, "To drift like clouds and flow like water." It is
strictly a Zen term. The Japanese word for Buddhist monks and priests
of all sects is bozu (bonze). One takes no formal vows upon becoming
an Unsui, although the head is shaved and a long Chinese-style robe
called koromo is worn within Sodo walls. Unsui are free to quit the
Zen community at any time. During the six months of the year in which
the Sodo is in session (spring and fall) they eat no meat, but during the
summer and winter off-periods they eat, drink and wear what they will.
After becoming temple priests (Osho, Chinese Ho-shang), the great
majority of Zen monks marry and raise families. The present generation
of young Unsui is largely from temple families.

44

priests of Shokoku-ji temples. A few, after years of zazen (meditation), koan study,[2] and final mastery of the Avatamsaka (Kegon) philosophy, become Roshi[3] (Zen Masters), qualified to head Sodos, teach lay groups, or do what they will. Laymen are also permitted to join the Unsui in evening Zendo (meditation hall) sessions, and some, like the Unsui, are given a koan by the Roshi and receive regular sanzen—the fierce face-to-face moment where you spit forth truth or perish—from him. Thus being driven, through time and much zazen, to the very end of the problem.

In the routine of Sodo life, there are special weeks during the year in which gardening, carpentry, reading and such, are suspended, and the time given over almost entirely to zazen. During these weeks, called sesshin, "concentrating the mind"— sanzen is received two to four times a day and hours of zazen in the Zendo are much extended. Laymen who will observe the customs of Sodo life and are able to sit still are allowed to join in the sesshin. At Shokoku-ji, the spring sesshin is held the first week of May.

The sesshin starts in the evening. The participants circle in single file into the mat-floored Central Hall of the Sodo and sit in a double row in dim light. The Roshi silently enters, sits at the head, and everyone drinks tea, each fishing his own teacup out of the deep-sleeved black robe. Then the Jikijitsu—head

[2] Koans are usually short anecdotes concerning the incomprehensible and illogical behavior and language of certain key Chinese Zen Masters of the T'ang Dynasty. The koan assigned to the student is the subject of his meditation, and his understanding of it is the subject of sanzen, an interview with the Zen Master. Very advanced students are also required to relate koan-understanding to the intellectual concepts of Buddhist philosophy.

[3] Roshi. Literally, "old master"—Chinese Lao-shih. A Roshi is not simply a person who "understands" Zen, but specifically a person who has received the seal of approval from his own Zen Master and is his "Dharma heir." A person may comprehend Zen to the point that his Roshi will say he has no more to teach him, but if the Roshi does not feel the student is intellectually and scholastically equipped to transmit Zen as well, he will not permit him to be his heir. Most Roshi are Zen monks, but laymen and women have also achieved this title.

Unsui of the Zendo (a position which revolves among the older men, changing every six months)—reads in formal voice the rules of Zendo and sesshin, written in Sung Dynasty Sino-Japanese. The Roshi says you all must work very hard; all bow and go out, returning to the Zendo for short meditation and early sleep.

At three a.m. the Fusu (another older Zenbo who is in charge of finances and meeting people) appears in the Zendo ringing a hand-bell. Lights go on—ten-watt things tacked under the beams of a building lit for centuries by oil lamps—and everyone wordlessly and swiftly rolls up his single quilt and stuffs it in a small cupboard at the rear of his mat, leaps off the raised platform that rings the hall, to the stone floor, and scuffs out in straw sandals to dash icy water on the face from a stone bowl. They come back quickly and sit crosslegged on their zazen cushions, on the same mat used for sleeping. The Jikijitsu stalks in and sits at his place, lighting a stick of incense and beginning the day with the rifleshot crack of a pair of hardwood blocks whacked together and a ding on a small bronze bell. Several minutes of silence, and another whack is heard from the Central Hall. Standing up and slipping on the sandals, the group files out of the Zendo, trailing the Jikijitsu—who hits his bell as he walks—and goes down the roofed stone path, fifty yards long, that joins the Zendo and the Central Hall. Forming two lines and sitting on the mats, they begin to chant sutras. The choppy Sino-Japanese words follow the rhythm of a fish-shaped wooden drum and a deep-throated bell. They roar loud and chant fast. The Roshi enters and between the two lines makes deep bows to the Buddha-image before him, lights incense, and retires. The hard-thumping drum and sutra-songs last an hour, then suddenly stop and all return to the Zendo. Each man standing before his place, they chant the *Prajña-paramita-hridaya Sutra,* the Jikijitsu going so fast now no one can follow him. Then hoisting themselves onto the mats, they meditate. After half an hour a harsh bell-clang is heard from the Roshi's quarters. The Jikijitsu bellows "Getout!" and the

Zenbos dash out racing, feet slapping the cold stones and robes flying, to kneel in line whatever order they make it before the sanzen room. A ring of the bell marks each new entrance before the Roshi. All one hears from outside is an occasional growl and sometimes the whack of a stick. The men return singly and subdued from sanzen to their places.

Not all return. Some go to the kitchen, to light brushwood fires in the brick stoves and cook rice in giant black pots. When they are ready they signal with a clack of wood blocks, and those in the Zendo answer by a ring on the bell. Carrying little nested sets of bowls and extra-large chopsticks, they come down the covered walk. It is getting light, and at this time of year the azalea are blooming. The moss-floored garden on both sides of the walk is thick with them, banks under pine and maple, white flowers glowing through mist. Even the meal, nothing but salty radish pickles and thin rice gruel, is begun and ended by whacks of wood and chanting of short verses. After breakfast the Zenbos scatter: some to wash pots, others to mop the long wood verandas of the central hall and sweep and mop the Roshi's rooms or rake leaves and paths in the garden. The younger Unsui and the outsiders dust, sweep, and mop the Zendo.

The Shokoku-ji Zendo is one of the largest and finest in Japan. It is on a raised terrace of stone and encircled by a stone walk. Outside a long overhang roof and dark unpainted wood— inside round log posts set on granite footings—it is always cool and dark and very still. The floor is square slate laid diagonal. The raised wood platform that runs around the edge has mats for forty men. Sitting in a three-walled box that hangs from the center of the ceiling, like an overhead-crane operator, is a lifesize wood statue of the Buddha's disciple Kasyapa, his eyes real and piercing anyone who enters the main door. In an attached room to the rear of the Zendo is a shrine to the founder of Shokoku-ji, his statue in wood, eyes peering out of a dark alcove.

By seven a.m. the routine chores are done and the Jikijitsu invites those cleaning up the Zendo into his room for tea. The Jikijitsu and the Fusu both have private quarters, the Fusu lodging in the Central Hall and the Jikijitsu in a small building adjoining the Zendo. The chill is leaving the air, and he slides open the paper screens, opening a wall of his room to the outside. Sitting on mats and drinking tea they relax and smoke and quietly kid a little, and the Jikijitsu—a tigerish terror during the zazen sessions—is very gentle. "You'll be a Roshi one of these days" a medical student staying the week said to him. "Not me, I can't grasp koans," he laughs, rubbing his shaved head where the Roshi has knocked him recently. Then they talk of work to be done around the Sodo. During sesshin periods work is kept to a minimum, but some must be done. Taking off robes and putting on ragged old dungarees everyone spreads out, some to the endless task of weeding grass from the moss garden, others to the vegetable plots. The Jikijitsu takes a big mattock and heads for the bamboo-grove to chop out a few bamboo shoots for the kitchen. Nobody works very hard, and several times during the morning they find a warm place in the sun and smoke.

At ten-thirty they quit work and straggle to the kitchen for lunch, the main meal. Miso-soup full of vegetables, plenty of rice and several sorts of pickles. The crunch of bicycles and shouts of children playing around the belltower can be heard just beyond the wall. After lunch the laymen and younger Unsui return to the Zendo. More experienced men have the greater responsibilities of running the Sodo, and they keep busy at accounts, shopping and looking after the needs of the Roshi. Afternoon sitting in the Zendo is informal—newcomers take plenty of time getting comfortable, and occasionally go out to walk and smoke a bit. Conversation is not actually forbidden, but no one wants to talk.

Shortly before three, things tighten up and the Jikijitsu comes in. When everyone is gathered, and a bell heard from the Central Hall, they march out for afternoon sutra-chanting. The

sutras recited vary from day to day, and as the leader announces
new titles some men produce books from their sleeves to read
by, for not all have yet memorized them completely. Returning
to the Zendo, they again recite the *Prajña-paramita-hridaya
Sutra,* and the Jikijitsu chants a piece alone, his voice filling the
hall, head tilted up to the statue of Kasyapa, hand cupped to his
mouth as though calling across miles.

After sitting a few minutes the signal is heard for evening
meal, and all file into the kitchen, stand, chant, sit, and lay out
their bowls. No one speaks. Food is served with a gesture of
"giving," and one stops the server with a gesture of "enough."
At the end of the meal—rice and pickles—a pot of hot water is
passed and each man pours some into his bowls, swashes it
around and drinks it, wipes out his bowls with a little cloth.
Then they are nested again, wrapped in their cover, and
everyone stands and leaves.

It is dusk and the Zendo is getting dark inside. All the Zenbos
begin to assemble now, some with their cushions tucked under
arm, each bowing before Kasyapa as he enters. Each man, right
hand held up before the chest flat like a knife and cutting the
air, walks straight to his place, bows toward the center of the
room, arranges the cushions, and assumes the crosslegged
"half-lotus" posture. Other arrive too—teachers, several college
professors and half a dozen university students wearing the
black uniforms that serve for classrooms, bars and temples
equally well—being all they own. Some enter uncertainly and
bow with hesitation, afraid of making mistakes, curious to try
zazen and overwhelmed by the historical weight of Zen,
something very "Japanese" and very "high class." One student,
most threadbare of all, had a head shaved like an Unsui and
entered with knowledge and precision every night, sitting
perfectly still on his cushions and acknowledging no one. By
seven-thirty the hall is half full—a sizable number of people for
present-day Zen sessions—and the great bell in the belltower
booms. As it booms, the man ringing it, swinging a long
wood-beam ram, sings out a sutra over the shops and homes of

the neighborhood. When he has finished, the faint lights in the Zendo go on and evening zazen has begun.

The Jikijitsu sits at the head of the hall, marking the half-hour periods with wood clackers and bell. He keeps a stick of incense burning beside him, atop a small wood box that says "not yet" on it in Chinese. At the end of the first half-hour he claps the blocks once and grunts "kinhin." This is "walking zazen," and the group stands—the Unsui tying up sleeves and tucking up robes—and at another signal they start marching single file around the inside of the hall. They walk fast and unconsciously in step, the Jikijitsu leading with a long samurai stride. They circle and circle, through shadow and under the light, ducking below Kasyapa's roost, until suddenly the Jikijitsu claps his blocks and yells "Getout!"—the circle broken and everyone dashing for the door. Night sanzen. Through the next twenty minutes they return to resume meditation—not preparing an answer now, but considering the Roshi's response.

Zazen is a very tight thing. The whole room feels it. The Jikijitsu gets up, grasps a long flat stick and begins to slowly prowl the hall, stick on shoulder, walking before the rows of sitting men, each motionless with eyes half-closed and looking straight ahead downward. An inexperienced man sitting out of balance will be lightly tapped and prodded into easier posture. An Unsui sitting poorly will be without warning roughly knocked off his cushions. He gets up and sits down again. Nothing is said. Anyone showing signs of drowsiness will feel a light tap of the stick on the shoulder. He and the Jikijitsu then bow to each other, and the man leans forward to receive four blows on each side of his back. These are not particularly painful—though the loud whack of them can be terrifying to a newcomer—and serve to wake one well. One's legs may hurt during long sitting, but there is no relief until the Jikijitsu rings his bell. The mind must simply be placed elsewhere. At the end of an hour the bell does ring and the second kinhin begins—a welcome twenty minutes of silent rhythmic walking. The walking ends abruptly and anyone not seated and settled when the Jikijitsu whips around the hall is knocked off his cushion. Zen aims at freedom but its practice is disciplined.

Several Unsui slip out during kinhin. At ten they return— they can be heard coming, running full speed down the walk. They enter carrying big trays of hot noodles, udon, in large lacquer bowls. They bow to the Jikijitsu and circle the room setting a bowl before each man; giving two or even three bowls to those who want them. Each man bows, takes up chopsticks, and eats the noodles as fast as he can. Zenbos are famous for fast noodle-eating and no one wants to be last done. As the empty bowls are set down they are gathered up and one server follows, wiping the beam that fronts the mats with a rag, at a run. At the door the servers stop and bow to the group. It bows in return. Then one server announces the person—usually a friend or patron of the Sodo—who footed the bill for the sesshin noodles that night. The group bows again. Meditation is resumed. At ten-thirty there is another rest period and men gather to smoke and chat a little in back. "Are there really some Americans interested in Zen?" they ask with astonishment—for their own countrymen pay them scant attention.

At eleven bells ring and wood clacks, and final sutras are chanted. The hall is suddenly filled with huge voices. The evening visitors take their cushions and leave, each bowing to the Jikijitsu and Kasyapa as he goes. The others flip themselves into their sleeping quilts immediately and lie dead still. The Jikijitsu pads once around, says, "Take counsel of your pillow," and walks out. The hall goes black. But this is not the end, for as soon as the lights go out, everyone gets up again and takes his sitting cushion, slips outside, and practices zazen alone wherever he likes for another two hours. The next day begins at three a.m.

This is the daily schedule of the sesshin. On several mornings during the week, the Roshi gives a lecture (teisho) based on some anecdote in the Zen textbooks—usually from *Mumonkan* or *Hekiganroku*. As the group sits in the Central Hall awaiting his entrance, one Zenbo stands twirling a stick around the edge-tacks of a big drum, filling the air with a deep reverberation. The Roshi sits crosslegged on a very high chair, receives a cup of tea, and delivers lectures that might drive some mad—for he tells these poor souls beating their brains out night after night that "the Perfect Way is without difficulty" and he means it and they know he's right.

In the middle of the week everyone gets a bath and a new head-shave. There is a Zen saying that "while studying koans you should not relax even in the bath," but this one is never heeded. The bathhouse contains two deep iron tubs, heated by brushwood fires stoked below from outside. The blue smoke and sweet smell of crackling hinoki and sugi twigs, stuffed in by a fire-tender, and the men taking a long time and getting really clean. Even in the bathhouse you bow—to a small shrine high on the wall—both before and after bathing. The Jikijitsu whets up his razor and shaves heads, but shaves his own alone and without mirror. He never nicks himself any more.

On the day after bath they go begging (takuhatsu). It rained this day, but putting on oiled-paper slickers over their robes and wearing straw sandals they splashed out. The face of the begging Zenbo can scarcely be seen, for he wears a deep bowl-shaped woven straw hat. They walk slowly, paced far apart, making a weird wailing sound as they go, never stopping. Sometimes they walk for miles, crisscrossing the little lanes and streets of Kyoto. They came back soaked, chanting a sutra as they entered the Sodo gate, and added up a meager take. The rain sluiced down all that afternoon, making a green twilight inside the Zendo and a rush of sound.

The next morning during tea with the Jikijitsu, a college professor who rents rooms in one of the Sodo buildings came in and talked of koans. "When you understand Zen, you know that the tree is really *there*."—The only time anyone said anything of Zen philosophy or experience the whole week. Zenbos never discuss koans or sanzen experience with each other.

The sesshin ends at dawn on the eighth day. All who have participated gather in the Jikijitsu's room and drink powdered green tea and eat cakes. They talk easily, it's over. The Jikijitsu, who has whacked or knocked them all during the week, is their great friend now—compassion takes many forms.

TANKER NOTES

At Sea   29: VIII: 57

Picked up rucksack, saw hospital and immigration, & was
took on launch to this ship, "Sappa Creek"—rusty and gray—
covered with pipes and valves and shit, standing on fantail
Mt. Fuji, the "new hip moon," Venus. In purple sunset. &
below to the engine room to my work, Fireman. Tending seven
red-eyed fires—roar and heat and sweat, jumble of pipes and
valves. Up once for a break out of the noise and heat to cool
air of fantail—Pleiades rising astern. Waves and machinery
and music, bulkheads and drying overalls and underwears. Why
all this oil? Ancient jungly heat of the sun.

— — — —

Jack the Wiper: Japanese whores are the kindest, cleanest, in
the world. And Goddammit, you really can't ever understand
them or can they you.

— — — —

Eight black pipe breasts with little alloy nipples, squirting flame.

— — — —

(Rape of the world: destructiveness of Western civilization.
Those insane Spaniards in Central America—answering to
abstractions of gold and religion. The nature, wildlife, Indian

life, Mississippi, Grand Canyon, didn't move them. The whole
Western hemisphere a gift to Spain from the Pope.)

– – – –

Off Singapore   6: IX

   Flying fish and a few bob-tailed shoreside-looking birds.
Pulled a hot one today and sprayed hot oil around the fire-room.
Now they say I'm a real fireman.

– – – –

Caruso the Oiler was "living in jungles and on Salvation Army
handouts" before he got this job. Now gone nuts over money
and madly saving, spending nothing, because he wants to
"leave an estate." His clothes are all beat up and he wanders
about with a distracted little smile. Last night Singapore in a
sudden cloudburst—nothing but a string of lights half-lost in
rain. This morning the coast of Malaya—a low beach with low
rugged hills behind it and tatters of cloud. Enter the Bay of
Bengal.
           —red wheel pipe-valves, silver-painted pipe elbows,
pumps flows and checks. Red, black, aluminum. Water
and oil. What curious forms love takes. Here in the belly
of a whale.

– – – –

Bengal Bay   nine nine

   White's father was a Spanish-American war soldier from
Maine who stayed on in the Philippines. "He made all kinds of
kids." Now in an old soldier's home in Monterey.
                "It's my desire to become President in

spite of the fact I wear second-hand clothes and say fuck every
3rd word"
Everyone working 12, 14, 16 hours a day—
all the overtime you want on this ship—and cherishing
each their fantasies of how to spend it. Sandy says "You'll
waste it all in whorehouses and bars." Then the cook says that
women are no good after twenty-nine, they start getting
female troubles, you can't fuck them the way you want, and
they start going to Preachers.

－－－－

Trincomalee Ceylon   12: IX

   Woke early on my cot on the boatdeck & saw a bird flash in,
soaring around the trees on shore—archaic planet epochs,
bird-and-rock dawn, mountain and ocean feeling—curiously
absent in Japan. Yesterday, coming into port, balancing
burners and pressures and watching frantic wobbly gauges.
British sailors with long blonde hair, in shorts.
   Ashore up oil-&-pipe pier to drink Ceylon beer with
Suquamish Indian Mason, & two beards Sandy & Jack. They on
watch but drinking beer for coffee-time. Then walkt alone
up hillside—scrubby dry sort of tough-leaved trees. Overlooking
China Bay, oil tanks and rusty railroads, corrugated sheds
and Tamil-speaking workmen. At a fresh-water storage
place two monkeys jumped from way high and land WHAP on
hard concrete, scampered off to the jungle, curly tails up high.

－－－－

   Poems that spring out fully armed; and those that are the
result of artisan care. The contrived poem, workmanship;
a sense of achievement and pride of craft; but the pure
inspiration flow leaves one with a sense of gratitude and

wonder, and no sense of "I did it"—only the Muse. *That* level
of mind—the cool water—not intellect and not—(as romantics
and after have confusingly thought) fantasy-dream world
or unconscious. This is just the clear spring—it reflects all
things and feeds all things but is of itself transparent. Hitting
on it, one could try to trace it to the source; but that writes
no poems and is in a sense ingratitude. Or one can see where it
goes: to all things and in all things. The hidden water
underground. Anyhow—one shouts for the moon in always
insisting on it; and safer-minded poets settle for any muddy flow
and refine it as best they can.

(Shaman poems: using mantra and mudra as well—)

– – – –

Midway   1: X: 57

   blue water breaking on the reef circle out there—white
flat island with ironwood trees like feathery pine; fairy tern
and long-tailed Tropic birds in the sky—and navy streets of
gray buildings. Hawaiian Dredge Co. men with helmets &
trucks, lift-trucks, steamrollers, dozers; yards of steel
reinforcing, tar, building materials by the acre.
   Drinking in the workers hall—dice games going—bearded
Hawaiian-Chinese-Japanese mixtures in rubber zori and hacked
off trouser shorts. Sitting across from Caruso, wood table,
cans of beer—the worst thing, he says, is greed. "Look at me—
greed ruined my life. Every time I see something I think
I got to have it. But the more you grab the farther it gets away."
Which advice in all humbleness I accept. & this morning,
sense of presence as I stepped into the quonset Catholic chapel
to scan the pamphlet rack; involuntary gassho and bow
to the virgin.
   White Terns—with delicate wing—and jetblack beak playing
in the evening through boughs of ironwood. Shell of a dead

tortoise. Body of a Frigate bird. Our own tracks seen
again in the sand.

———

five seamen in a coil of dirty hawser
smoke and rest and talk

———

Happy in the valves and oil leaks pipe checks gauge tubes light
bulbs blowers bilge pumps stools guards brushes marine
plugs & boat drills.
only the great wall of China could be seen
from the moon
"You talkin about the S.U.P.—that's a fuckin fink union all
the way down the line."

———

At Sea   Arabian Sea   6: XI

Passed a small neat slow Russian tanker.
Scraping down the deck of the steering-gear room.

"man, she was rough.
selling blood to get something to eat.
Galveston."

Jack defends liquor (Perschke)—"I like to drink, man it makes
me feel good—I like to stagger from one bar to another—I
don't give a shit about *anything*—somebody asks me for my
shirt, I give it to them—I don't worry about *nothin*." Duperont
the Cook says, "Somebody drunk he's runnin away from
somethin—cain't hide behind a bottle forever."

———

Three of the four Arab boatmen riding through the
canal on the fantail—warm up hashish with kerosene, make a
hookah with jar and bamboo tubes, keep it burning with a
charcoal ember, and pass it around. The oldest passes it with
a huge laugh. "He's higher than a Georgia pine" says
Perschke. The Arabs have three tables in the messhall covered
with wares—rough switchblade knives, camel-quirts,
Turkish Delight, pencils with Egyptian stencils.

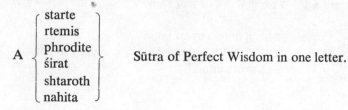

A
starte
rtemis
phrodite
śirat
shtaroth
nahita

Sūtra of Perfect Wisdom in one letter.

- - - -

Joe the Chief Cook—a SANE man—says of the captain,
"Maybe I can't outsmart the cocksucker, but I can outDUMB
him"

- - - -

At Sea   29: XI

Jack's wino days in Galveston—stealing blankets from
whores and sleeping in parked cars. "Marriage—that's WEAK!"
he shouts. "Somebody's got to keep the whores and
bartenders from going broke."   "THAT cocksucker—telling
me I ought to save money—feast or famine! I'll be walking
along shaky with wine, broke, with a beard, no place to
sleep, and see a guy with his wife and kids, and think how lucky
I am."   "Wakin up in the morning in the weeds, sleepin

on my belly, parting the grass with my hands looking
for a wine-jug——peering & peering."

—— —— —— ——

At Sea   Arabian Sea   8: XII

Duperont's first job—age nine—"A man said he'd give
me five dollars if I'd wash a daid man. Well bring his dead ass
here & I'll wash hell out of it, I said."

Caruso: "It's a long way to Suez"
Duperont: "It ain't a long way man, it's just you got
              a short mind."

—— —— —— ——

"The Gulf crews are good but men from Mobile are wild—
Boston seamen are gashounds and performers—twenty years ago
the West Coast had good crews——"

—— —— —— ——

Iskenderun, Turkey   20: XII: 57

Jesse the Guamanian and I sit waiting for our friends
outside a whorehouse, in the afternoon. Eucalyptus trees and
pines, hordes of sparrows. Great muddy yard, small horses
everywhere. Charcoal braziers. After the ladies, (one was an
aristocratic slender Negro about fifty with streaks of silver
in her hair) rode back to a dead restaurant and drank cheap
sweet wine.
10-year-old raggedy-dress barelegged blonde girl comes
down the sidewalk (I'm standing across the street digging sunset
and people going homeward)—with smaller children—

all holding hands—making a small ring, and dancing a thing
as they come, wheeling,   the girl kicks up a leg and
WHOOPS at the two horses waiting at the curb; laughs at their
start; and on her way.

Istanbul   25: XII

Woke sleeping on the floor in a hotel room—Bos'n &
Chief Cook on the bed. Got outside and found a place to eat,
all soup and bread in a mutton-smelling room; soup dashed with
vinegar. Then found a map and worked my way up the hills
and alleys to Hagia Sophia. What emptiness, what coolness. I
was alone in it. Mary and child mosaic—shivering and
half-crying, the image of lost ceremony, heart and splendor,
once hanging lamps and echoing chants beneath the dome.

Back through Suez   4: I: 58

Duperont on Galveston before the war—"Them whores was
flying about like dead leaves."   "—Don't want no beauty
in a woman; that's just a lot of war-paint and charcoal and them
eyes drawed back like Fu Manchu and all them ropes and
chains dangling from their arms, I see right through all that."

Perschke on girls: "I couldn't pick up a blind owl."

Duperont on virginity—"Virginity, a woman spend years
protectin that little bit of cherry and she lose it in a minute.
What kind of nonsense is that? And after they lose it

61

they're kicking themselves for not startin fifteen years sooner
and then pretty soon they're boo-hooing that they're getting old
and start patting that shit on their faces and peering about
for wrinkles."   and, "Ninety percent of these poor
cocksuckers fucked up in the haid.   Ain't nothin like peace of
mind."

A higher sense of responsibility to holy ghosts and foolishness
and mess.   (The Chinese shot: A young man's love
for a girl; an old man viewing nature.)

———

At Sea

          talking with Perschke on the fantail. I ask him
"What time do you go on lookout?"
—"When the sun sets. But I can't tell tonight, it's
     cloudy."
—"In Japan in the Buddhist temples they ring the evening
     bell when it gets so dark you can't see the lines in
     your hand while sitting in your room."
—"Full length or up close?"
—"Full length I guess."
—"Suppose you got a long arm. Maybe you're late. Are the
     windows open?"
—"Don't have any windows. The walls are open."
—"Always?"
—"Sometimes they're closed."
—"Can't always ring it at the right time, huh. What do
     they ring it for anyway."
—"Wake people up."
—"But that's in the evening."
—"They ring it in the morning too."

———

Reaching through hot pipes to turn nuts—the burned arm—
squiggle lines and tiny surprise silver tube running off somewhere
to tweet a gauge—box wrench $^{13}/_{16}$; eye beam you beam,
bulkhead sweat—flange leak and valve drip—old gasket pounder
—poke the big bolt through, seek nuts in pocket—whole ship
twined about us, where do the pipes go? The engineer
cursing and burning his unsteady hand—

————

18: II: 58   heading back into the Persian Gulf

Dark little tanker scoots under the sunset-black hills of
Muscat, her two lights on.
Jessie's tale: "Put it in" she said. "It's in already"
I said. "Ooh, it hurts."

————

Ras Tanura   20: II: 58

At dawn fixing the steering gear—ruddershaft packing and
driveshaft packing. Oslo ship next pier. Lateen rig open
small boat brisking by, a light rain on the green water,
ancient Sumer. The wheezy bang-headed rib-busted half-dead
gashound second cook we picked up in Okinawa was removed on
account of kidney stones. I think he found us an uncongenial
crew—eccentric and unwarm to strangers.
                              Beach shallowing
out in light green offing. Gulls squabbling, little tender
baby gulls amidst them.
          Amber spray of coffee in the sun flung from the deck
to the green foam. Gannets around here too.

Jesse says on Guam the women take "lemon leaf and abas" and boil it, and then "sit on it" and wash out with it—after childbirth—to make cunnus come back tight. Thus, Jesse says, a woman can have any number of babies and always be like new.

— — — —

"I love you all
I want the whole
World to know
Except my wife"

                              Jesus Evaristo

writ on the blackboard—crew mess.

— — — —

At Sea   20: III: 58

Cleaning, greasing, & labeling bearings. Hoover, New Departure, SKF, MRC, Federal. Shades of Bernhard Karlgren. A sunset of cloud-levels and alleys; hundred-miles-off cumulus peaks. The North Star sunk clean out of sight.
——madly singing and laughing, perched on pipes high on the shipside painting lower engine-room white—this is what I was born for——

— — — —

21:III   At Sea   Meridian Day: noon 13° 47S; 174° 47 W

Pago Pago, Samoa   23: III

Saturday morning woke to see green hills close by and a rough white surf on a steep beach. Ship swings into a small

gap that opened into the crescent harbor—a high steep
twin-peaked hill at the mouth, and white bungalows about.
Six destroyers waiting for us at a pier. Docked in, Samoan men
skirted & wearing heavy brown belts, with tough thick bare
feet. Japanese tuna boats anchored farther back.

Had to open up a manhole cover on main motor air cooler—
then got money and went ashore—a crowd of Samoans
waiting at inter-island steamer. Everyone so beautiful; went to
postoffice and bought stamps from tall lovely girl, wandered
in zori and already being swallowed in lotus-eater air down to
grass square where boys played baseball, ringed with little
buildings. Steep hill behind and mad blossoming flowers
everywhere. A policeman told me where a cheap bar was, but I
persisted toward Pago bar where shipmates are said to be.
There found Crazy Horse and Charley—beer in cans—and
had another policeman quick befriend me, saying he hated
having his policeman shirt on because people wouldn't
talk to him ("My father was a policeman and he told me not
to be a policeman, you have too many enemies") so I took
off shirt that John the second cook had passed on to me when
Yon the messman was took off the ship in Ras Tanura,
and gave it him.

Then danced wildly and clumsily, barechested, with Samoan
girls. Cop warned me about these girls and said he'd take
me to his house that night for food and friends. But in spite
of kind advice, when this girl sat down beside me and took my
hand, while reading letters—then she said "kiss me"—I did,
then she read her letters, then she said "I be your girl"
—I said O.K. then she said "kiss me" I did. Then she read
more letters. One addressed "Joanie Talofaa" the other
"Janie Talofaa." I said What's your name? She said "Janie."
I said, that other letter says "Joanie." "Yes" she said,
my name's "Joanie." —but you said your name was Janie.
"—It's all the same."

I dance about with her, then with other girls. Finally

she gets peeved some. The policeman is disgusted with me and left (later to find Perschke and give him many nice things, mats etc.—which Jack ultimately forgot) and I got drunker and ended up in back room on a mat-bed; Henricks also there him with Joanie's girl friend Sally who was eight months pregnant (several pregnant fillies around—still working the incoming seamen)—I made weird scene with another girl, which annoyed Joanie. Sitting out back of Pago bar. Bos'n coming out to piss, dead drunk, and falling down inside a trucktire asswise and stuck, couldn't get out.

Sometime I had gone back to the ship and gotten another shirt. Then we went to the beach—girls making us buy lots of stupid food—soda pop, half-case of beer, etc. Long taxi ride to place by an old airstrip; a piece of shallow beach with reef far out. The pantryman, oiler, and Jr. Third were also there. I had blankets and rucksack picked up from ship. Ate island style with fingers, breaking bread and grabbing food—a little kid came along and we traded canfood for some steamed breadfruit. Joanie decided to swim, stripped to panties and went in. I started a fire, but it was too windy and not much firewood. The place looked like a dirty old picnic ground—the Samoans had no qualms about tossing tincans helterskelter, which did bug me. The feeling of let-go when you get here! My mind almost stopped working; pure intoxication and utter failure of willpower curiosities. Like Wong says, YOU JUST GO OFF YOUR HEAD IN PORT.

Then I went swimming and made love way out in the water, twilight, while she improvised a long song. Warm warm water. Go ashore and check trousers, which Joanie had moved, and $20 is missing. Either Joanie or the Third's girls had took em. Not much use in making a scene—I'd been warned. Then nap under blanket, more lovemaking, and learning elaborate Polynesian customs. 4 a. m. cab came back and we return to ship, quarreling and shouting.

Down the gangplank comes Wong mean and sore and trying

to find his lost wallet. Joanie went back with the taxi and
tried to make it with the pumpman. Next morning I wandered
around—way down the lanes and back—old car garages,
a dead dog in a creek, crappers on pilings perched out over the
water. Complex structure of post-walled palm-leaf roofed
houses and fine patterned interiors done in process of lashing
posts and bent palm-log beams.

Ran into Joanie, Sally, Henricks—we all went to the Tuna
bar to drink and chaff; the First and the Chief also there—
then time to go back. Ship whistle blew. The four of us, two
girls, two seamen, walk back. Kiss goodbye; Joanie says
"ashamed" to do it in front of everybody—after we're all on
board, and the hawsers are off and the ship easing off the
pier, she goes out on a bungalow lawn, whips off her lava-lava
and waves it to us, then takes down her pants and bends
over her bare arse at the watching crew—man we laughed—she
turned around and presented us her snatch; then went. The
ship almost left behind Ambrosio L.G. Cruz; a launch pulled
him alongside and he came up the Jacob's ladder.

Kwajalein   30: III

Americans are splendid while working—attentive, cooperative,
with dignity and sureness—but the same ones seen later at
home or bar are sloppy, bored and silly. Japanese almost the
opposite—better at home than at work. (This when steering gear
was out and we were all trying to figure why the hydraulic
system wouldn't swing the rudder around. Air in the line.

Drinking with Joe: "If I'd 'v had education, I'd 'v been
a MOTHERFUCKER."

15: IV: 58   approaching San Pedro,

Five Laysan Albatrosses have followed us. The lights of
San Pedro—seawater color changes, the air smell is different, the
Albatrosses turn back, and the seagulls come to escort the
tanker in.

RECORD OF THE LIFE OF THE CH'AN MASTER PO-CHANG HUAI-HAI

[Bojang Whyhigh]

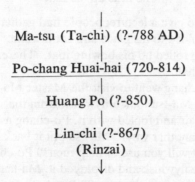

Ma-tsu (Ta-chi) (?-788 AD)

Po-chang Huai-hai (720-814)

Huang Po (?-850)

Lin-chi (?-867)
(Rinzai)

background and youth

The Ch'an Master Huai-hai of Po-chang mountain in
Hung-chou was from Ch'ang-lo in Fu-chou. When he still
had his hair tied in knots, he split from society. He was
well-drilled in the "Three Studies" (morality, meditation and
wisdom). While Ma-tsu was teaching in Nan-k'ang,
Huai-hai whole-heartedly became his disciple.

Translated from the *Ching-tê Chuan-têng Lu,* "Transmission of the
Lamp" Ch. VI. Taisho Tripitaka 51.249b ff.

69

rivalry with Hsi-t'ang

Po-chang and Hsi-t'ang Chih-ts'ang were called
"room-entering" disciples. At that time these two fine yogins
were rivals in their Ch'an study. One evening the two
were with Ma-tsu at the harvest moon-watching. Ma-tsu
said, "When it's just like this, what about it?" Hsi-t'ang
replied, "A fine time to make an offering." Po-chang
said, "A fine time to practice." Ma-tsu commented—"The
sūtras went into Ts'ang/'Tripitaka'; meditation
returned into Hai/'Sea'."

he rolls up his mat

Ma-tsu was to give a lecture; people had gathered like
clouds. He ascended to his place and sat a while.
Then Po-chang rolled up his bowing mat. Thereupon
Ma-tsu left the hall.

One day Po-chang went to visit the Master Ma-tsu in
the lecture hall. Ma-tsu took a flywhisk from the
corner of his chair and fooled with it. Po-chang asked "Just
this, or is there another way?" Ma-tsu put it back saying
"After this what will you use to help men?" Po-chang
himself took the flywhisk and displayed it. Ma-tsu said
"Just this, or is there another way?" Po-chang hung
the flywhisk up, and waited. Ma-tsu shouted "K' AAA!"

he begins teaching

From that time on, his thunder reverberated. Sure
enough, some believers invited him to the Hsing-wu
district in Hung-chou, to live at Mt. Ta-hsiung. Since he
lived in a dangerously steep, mountainous place, they
called him "Po-chang" (Hundred Fathoms). Before he had
been there a full year, students of the profound treasure had
gathered like clouds from the four directions. Among
them, Kuei-shan and Huang-po became the leaders.

70

Po-chang and Huang-po

One day the master addressed the group: "The
Buddha-Dharma is not a small affair. I twice met with
the Great Master Ma's "K' AAA!" It deafened and blinded me
three days."

Huang-po hearing this, unconsciously stuck out his
tongue* saying "I don't know Ma-tsu, and after all
I never met him." The Master said "You'll be his heir
eventually." —"I won't be Ma-tsu's heir" Huang-po
replied. "Why?" "—Afterwards I'd have no descendants."
The Master said "That's so, that's so."

the crying comrade

One day a comrade came into the lecture hall
weeping. The Master said "What's up?" He replied "My
father and mother have both died. Will the Master
please set a date for their funeral service?" The Master said
"Come tomorrow and we'll bury them both at once."

speak without using your mouth

At lecture the Master said "Choke your throat, shut
your mouth, now quickly speak!" Kuei-shan said
"I won't, you speak!" The Master said "I don't refuse
to talk with you, but afterwards I'd have no heirs."
Wu-feng said "The Master also should shut up." The
Master said to him "If we were here alone, I'd be

---

* From here to the end of this anecdote the Ming version is as follows:
The Master said, "Aren't you going to become the heir of Ma-tsu?"
Huang-po said "Indeed not. Today, because of your exposition, I have
been able to see Ma-tsu's power in action. But I never knew him.
If I were to be Ma-tsu's heir, afterwards I'd have no descendants."
The Master said, "That's so, that's so. If your understanding is equal
to your teacher's, you diminish his power by half. Only if you surpass
your teacher, will you be competent to transmit. You are very well
equipped to surpass your teacher."

shading my eyes looking up at you." Yun-yen said "I also
have something to say. Please ask the question
again." "—Choke your throat, shut your mouth, speak
quickly!" "—Now the Master has it!" Po-chang
said: "I'll have no heirs."

who'll go to Hsi-t'ang?

The Master said to the group "I need someone to
carry a message to Hsi-t'ang, who'll go?"
Wu-feng said "Me." "—How are you going to
transmit the message?" Wu-feng said "When I see Hsi-t'ang
I'll tell him." "—What will you say?" "—When I
come back, I'll tell you."

is there fire or not

The Master and Kuei-shan were out working, and the
Master asked "Is there fire?" "—There is." "Where?"
Kuei-shan took a stick, blew on it two or three times and passed
it to Po-chang. "This worm-eaten stick!"

what is the Buddha like?

Someone asked "What's the Buddha?" and Po-chang said
"Who are you?" The Wayfarer said "Me." The Master said
"Do you know 'me'?" "Clearly." The Master lifted his
flywhisk, "Do you see?" "—I see." Po-chang said nothing
more.

the dinner drum

Once when everyone was working together hoeing, a
comrade heard the dinner drum and suddenly putting up his
mattock with a big laugh he left. Po-chang said "Brilliant!
This is the gate where Avalokiteśvara enters the Principle." The

72

Master returned to his quarters and sent for that comrade, asking, "What truth did you perceive just now to act thus?"   "—I just heard the dinner drum pounding and went back to eat." The Master laughed.

depending on the sūtras

Someone asked, "If we interpret in accordance with the sūtras, the Buddhas of the Three Worlds hate sūtras, every word, as though they were the chatter of demons. What about this?" Po-chang said "If we hang on tight to circumstances the Buddhas of the Three Worlds hate it; if we seek anywhere else outside this, it's the chatter of demons."

a comrade and Hsi-t'ang

A comrade asked Hsi-t'ang, "There is a question and there is an answer. What about it when there's no question or answer?" Hsi-t'ang said "You mean to say you're afraid of rotting?" The Master heard about this and said "I've always wondered about that fellow Hsi-t'ang." The comrade asked the Master to comment on it. He said "The world of phenomena is not to be perceived."

the hungry man and the full

The Master said to the community "There's a man who doesn't eat for a long time—but doesn't say he's starving; there's a man who eats every day but doesn't say he's full." No one could answer this.

the needy man

Yun-yen asked "For whom are you bustling about like this every day?" Po-chang replied "There's a man needs me." Yen said "Why don't you let him do it himself?"   "—He can't even make his own living."

A comrade asked "What about the Dharma-gate of Mahayana Sudden Enlightenment?" The Master said:

"All of you: first stop all causal relationships, and bring the ten thousand affairs to rest. Good or not good, out of the world or in the world—don't keep *any* of these dharmas in mind. Don't have causally conditioned thoughts. Relinquish both body and mind and make yourself free, with a mind like wood or stone—making no discriminations. Then the mind is without action, and the mind-ground is like the empty sky. Then the sun of wisdom will appear by itself, like clouds opening and the sun coming out. Completely stop all involving causes: greed, anger, lust, attachment. Feelings of purity or impurity should be extinguished. As for the five desires and the eight lusts, one need not be bound by seeing, hearing, perceiving or knowing; or be deluded under any circumstance. Then you will be endowed with supernatural and mysterious power. Thus is the liberated man.

As for all kinds of circumstances, the mind of such a man is without either tranquillity or disorder—neither concentrated or scattered. Then there is no obstruction to the complete comprehension of Sound and Form. Such may be called a man of Tao. He is bound in no way by good or bad, purity or impurity, or the uses of worldly happiness and wisdom. This is what we call Buddha-Wisdom. Right and wrong, pretty and ugly, reasonable and unreasonable—all intellectual discriminations are completely exhausted. Being unbound, his mental condition is free. Such a man may be called a Bodhisattva whose Bodhi-mind arrives the instant it sets out. Such can ascend directly to the Buddha lands.

All the dharmas, basically, are not of themselves empty. They do not, themselves, speak of form; also they say nothing of right and wrong or purity and impurity; and they have no intention of binding men. The fact is that men themselves deludedly speculate and make several kinds of understanding and bring forth several kinds of intellectual discrimination. If feelings of purity and impurity could be exhausted, if one didn't dwell in attachments and didn't dwell in liberation— if there were absolutely no drawing-of-lines between conditioned and unconditioned—if the mind analyzed without making choices—THEN THAT MIND WOULD BE FREE. One would not be tangled up with illusion, suffering, the skandhas, samsara or the twelve links of the chain. Remote, unattached, completely without clinging. Going or staying without obstruction; entering into or coming out of Birth-and-Death is like going through opening gates. Even when that mind meets with various sorts of suffering and things that go wrong, that mind does not retreat groveling.

Such a one is not concerned with fame, clothing or food. He doesn't covet merit or profit; he is not obstructed by social things. Though he may be brought up against pleasure or pain, he doesn't get involved. Coarse food sustains his life, patched clothes resist the weather. He is vacant, like a complete idiot or deaf man.

If one has the least inclination toward broadly studying Understanding within samsara—seeking fortune and wisdom— it will add nothing to the Principle. Instead one will be hung up by the circumstances of understanding; and return to the sea of samsara. Buddha is an unseekable One: if you seek it you go astray. The Principle is an unseekable Principle; if you seek it you lose it. And if you manage not to seek, it turns to seeking. This Dharma has neither substance or emptiness. If you are able to flow through life with a mind as open and complete as wood or stone— then you will not be swept away and drowned by the skandhas, the five desires and the eight lusts. Then the source of Birth-and-Death will be cut off, and you will go and come freely.

You will not in the least be bound by the conditions of karma. With an unfettered body you can share your benefits with all things. With an unfettered mind you can respond to all minds.

With an unfettered wisdom you can loosen all bonds.
You are able to give the medicine according to the disease.

the comrade who had received precepts

A comrade asked, "Now that I have taken these precepts
my body and mouth are pure—I have already possessed
only the good—have I not achieved liberation?" Po-chang
said "To some degree you are liberated. But you are not yet
mentally liberated. You don't yet have complete liberation." The
comrade asked "What's mental liberation?" "—Don't seek
Buddha or understanding; exhaust feelings of pure and
impure. Also don't hold on to this non-seeking as right. Don't
dwell where you exhaust feelings, either. Don't dread the
chains of Hell and don't love the pleasures of Paradise.
Don't cling to any dharma whatsoever. Then you may begin
to be called liberated without hindrance; then body and
mind and *all* may be called liberated.

You shouldn't say you have a small part of the good of the
precepts, and take it to be enough. Though you may have
mastered the countless-as-river-sands purities of the gates of
Morality, Meditation and Wisdom, you have not yet touched
on a fraction of an atom of it. Strive courageously and get down
to work. Don't wait until your ears are blocked, your eyes
clouded, your hair white and your face wrinkled; your body
aged and suffering and your eyes filled with water; your mind
filled with anxiety, and no place to go. When you get to that
point you won't be able to even set your hands and feet in order.
Even though you have fortune, wisdom and much information,
it won't help you. Since the eye of your mind is not opened,
and your thinking is connected with circumstances, you will not
know how to reflect inwardly, and will be unable to see the
Buddha-way. Then all the karma of your whole life will appear
before you—whether it is pleasing or whether it is terrifying—
the Six Roads and the five skandhas all appear visible before
you. Because you have given reign to your own greediness what

you see will all be transformed into the highly desirable:
ornamenting houses, boats and carriages in glittering display.
Attaching importance to what you see, your rebirths will not be
free. Dragon, beast, freeman, slave—it's still all undecided."

The comrade asked "How do you get freedom?" The Master
answered "Now in regard to the five desires and eight lusts, have
no feelings of either acceptance or rejection. Let 'purity' and
'impurity' be completely exhausted. Like the sun and the moon
in the sky—shining without causal relationships. Have a mind
like wood or stone; or like the mind of Gandhahasti—who cut
the flow and went beyond, without obstruction. ₁Such a man
cannot be gathered in by either Heaven or Hell. Also, he
doesn't read the sūtras and scan teachings; language should
pliably return into oneself. All verbal teachings merely
illuminate his present understanding of his own nature. He is
in no way being revolved by the dharmas of existence or
non-existence. Such is a guiding master; able to see though all
the dharmas of existence and non-existence. Such is the
VAJRA.

Then he has his portion of freedom and independence. If he
cannot obtain it in this way, although he may be able to chant
the twelve Vedas he only becomes arrogant, and this is
slandering the Buddha, not a spiritual practice. From a worldly
standpoint, reading sūtras and observing the teachings is a good
thing; but from the standpoint of an illumined person it
obstructs men. Even a man who has mastered the Ten Stages
(Dasabhumi) cannot avoid flowing along in samsara's river.
There is no need to seek understanding via speech, values in
words. Understanding belongs to greed, and greed turns into
illness. If you can separate—right now—from all the dharmas
of being and non-being—and pass straight through the "Three
Phrases" then you will naturally be no different from the
Buddha. If you yourself are Buddha, why worry that Buddha
cannot speak? My only fear is that you are not Buddha, and
that you will be revolved by the dharmas of being and
non-being, and not be free. That is why, before Principle has

been established, you will be carried about by happiness and wisdom. It's like the slave employing the master. Better to establish Principle first, and later have happiness and wisdom.

At the proper time you'll get powers—you'll be able to take dirt and make gold, to turn seawater into buttermilk, to break Mount Sumeru down into dust; to take one meaning and make countless meanings; to take countless meanings and make one meaning."

The Master had finished his talk, and the community was leaving the hall. Then he called after them, and they all turned their heads. He called "What *is* this?"

Po-chang's death

In the ninth year of Yüan Ho, T'ang dynasty, on the seventeenth day of the first month, the Master returned to the silence. He was ninety-five.

In the first year of the Ch'ang-ch'ing era (821 AD) he was given the Imperially-conferred posthumous title of "Ta-chih Ch'an Master." His stupa was titled "Great Precious Excelling Wheel."

The Regulations of the Ch'an Line

The Ch'an line, from the time of its founding by Bodhidharma, to the Sixth Patriarch, and on up to the time of Po-chang, usually made its quarters in the temples of the Vinaya sect. Although it had separate buildings, there was yet no agreement on rules concerning teaching and administration. The Ch'an Master Po-chang Ta-chih, constantly concerned about this, said: "The Way of the Patriarchs should be one of expanding and transforming mankind. We hope that it will not die out in the future. Why should we accord our practices with every detail of the Agamas (Theravada Vinaya rules)?"

78

Someone said, "The *Yoga-śastra* and the *Ying-lo Ching* contain the Mahayana regulations. Why not follow them!" Po-chang said "What I follow isn't bound by the Great or Small Vehicles, and doesn't differentiate between them. We must strike a balance between the broad and the narrow, and establish rules that are suitable."

Thereupon, beginning a new idea, he established entirely different meditation dwellings.

In the community, everyone whose Dharma-eye is respectably powerful is called "Chang-lao" just as in India men of age and understanding were called "Subhuti," etc. After they have become "Transformers" or "Refiners" they live in the fang-chang room. Like Vimalakirti's room, it is without individual bedrooms. The reason that we build lecture halls, but no Buddha-halls, is to show that the Buddhas and Patriarchs personally appoint the Masters even today, and it is they who become the "Buddha."

Students enter the Comrades' Hall, without distinction of many or few, high or low. In order of how many seasons they've spent, they arrange and set up long connected benches and put up clothes racks to hang their equipment on. They sleep with their pillows leaned against the edge of the bench, on the auspicious right side of the body, because they do zazen for long hours, and need a little rest. Thus they have all the Four Dignities (standing, sitting, walking and lying down).

Aside from entering the Master's room to receive the teaching, students are permitted to be diligent or idle; the high and the low are not bound to a common rule. This whole group has study in the morning and an assembly in the evening. When the old chief ascends his high seat and gives a lecture, the leaders and the group stand in rows listening. The "Guest" and the "Host" trade questions and answers to display the principles of the Dharma—to display how they follow and live by the Dharma.

Meals are held twice a day at suitable times, because it is necessary to be frugal, and to show that Dharma and food go together. When working outside, those of high and those of low rank work equally hard.

Po-chang established ten offices and called them "liao-she" ("huts"). Each office has one man as chief, who is in charge of a number of men who each look after the affairs of their own department.

> Item: the man in charge of cooking is called "The rice head."
> The man in charge of vegetables is called "The greens head." The others all follow this pattern.

If there is someone who has falsely taken the name and stolen the form of a comrade, muddying the pure community and obstructing its affairs, then the welfare worker (Wei-na) investigates, removes his nameplate and clothes rack, and has him leave the grounds. The reason for this is to preserve the peace of the community. If that person has actually transgressed in some serious way then he should be beaten with a staff; assemble the group and burn his robe, bowls and equipment, and chase him out by a side gate. This shows his disgrace. Being particular about this one custom has four advantages: First, not muddying the pure community will give birth to reverence and faith.

> Item: if the three inheritances (word, deed and thought) are not good, men cannot live together. In accordance with the customs it is sometimes appropriate to use the "Brahma Altar" method to regulate someone [ostracizing an offender with total silence]. Some persons must be thrown out of the community— when the community is tranquil, reverence and faith will grow.

Secondly, the forms of the comrades are not destroyed, and the Buddhist precepts are complied with.

> Item: punish offenders properly, if they were allowed to keep their robes you'd regret it later.

Third, this way you don't trouble the law courts, and you keep out of criminal litigation. Fourth, it doesn't leak to outsiders—this protects the harmony of the tradition.

Item: when people come from all over to live together, what distinguishes the common man and the sage? Even when the Tathagata was in the world there were six classes of common monks; how much more today, in the decline of the Dharma, we cannot hope to have absolutely none. If one comrade commits an error, and all the other comrades make accusations, they surely don't realize that they are demeaning the community and destroying the Dharma; how great this destruction is. If the Ch'an group of these days wishes to move without hindrance, we must rely on Po-chang's Thick Grove regulations to manage affairs. Furthermore, it is not on account of the worthy ones that we set up a law guarding against transgressions. It is better to have rules and no faults, than it is to have faults and no rules. With Master Po-chang's protection, the Dharma has flourished and grown!

That the Ch'an Line is nowadays standing foremost can be traced to Po-chang. We have related the essentials and displayed them for comrades of future generations, that they forget not their roots. The complete rules are provided at all "Mountain Gates."

— — — —

I am indebted to Dr. Yoshitaka, IRIYA, Head of the Chinese Department of Nagoya University, and Fellow of the Jimbun Kagaku Kenkyusho, Kyoto, for valuable help in this translation.

Note: The word usually translated "monk" in English is the Chinese *sêng*—meaning "a member of the *sêng-chia*"—Skt Saṇgha, Community. Thus "comrade" is a member of a "community" (Saṇgha).

A JOURNEY TO RISHIKESH & HARDWAR

Level green sugarcane fields north of Delhi a day's bus ride to Hardwar. Bus change and one more hour to Rishikesh. A two-rupee tonga-ride to the mouth of the gorge and Shivananda's ashram.

Allen Ginsberg, Peter Orlovsky, my wife Joanne and me—simple to travel in this group—Allen can go buy tickets and check times while Peter and I lift rucksacks up on the bus-top, and Joanne gets seats inside. Rishikesh is a small town on the flat just where the lower Himalayas, the Siwaliks, begin and the Ganges debouches from the hills onto the plain. Hardwar-Rishikesh and on up the Ganges gorge is all exceedingly holy territory. The area crops up in the *Jataka* tales as the home of mountain-dwelling rishis, magic monkeys and elephants and wide groves of mango trees.

We arrived at the Ashram 9:30 in the evening and were led into a basement under a semi-finished brick building full of people slouching cross-legged on the floor, perhaps one-third Westerners. A giant man in a camel's-hair coat on a sort of heart-saver couch intoning "OM . . . OM . . ." shaved face and head. We had come in at the end of the evening darshan, "presence." The helpers, guests, and disciples were now being served sweet hot milk and fried chick-peas. Shivananda asked us, "Do they have these (chick-peas) in the United States?" Allen Ginsberg answered, "Yes."

Shivananda was then half-lifted to his feet by two junior

swamis who helped him step by step walk out and to his room. He is over six feet and in his eighties—looks like an ex-wrestler, must have been a powerful vigorous man, to judge by the energy he exudes even when half-crippled. He was born in South India, educated as an M.D., practiced ten years in Malaya, then became a sannyasin at Rishikesh. After some years of yoga practice and study, started his Yoga-Vedanta Forest Academy Ashram around 1936.

Taken up the hill in back to "Mt. Kailash" on a gravelly trail by flashlight. Given a half-bucket of water. Sleeping bags on dusty cots and concrete floor.

Morning, water from the creek up the hill. Monkeys fight with dogs. A boy comes with a pot of hot tea "chai" and pours us out cups, 8 a.m. View southeast down the Ganges—soil on the steep hillside loose and scrabbly between wide-spaced broad-leafed evergreen trees. Across the river a forested three-thousand-foot hill with marks of a farm near the top.

Looking around the ashram, found the Shivananda Ayurvedic Homeopathic Medecine shop and bought some Swami Shivananda Toothpowder. It dyes the mouth red, tastes like gunpowder, and scratches. Lunch in the dining hall sitting on the floor, eating off flat trays, use the right hand only; usual vegetarian sort, only less. Then told we would have to leave the ashram the following day because a crowd of guests was expected for Shivaratri, Shiva's Night—but that we could find lodgings across the Ganges at the Swarg Ashram, really a hostel —no teacher and no program.

That night at darshan, Shivananda gives us (sitting mingled in the crowd) each an envelope containing Rupees five. A series of young swamis got up to read or recite inspirational literature —both English and Hindi—a kind of amateur hour, for Shivananda would cut them off when he got bored, saying, "OM . . . ."

Shivananda on himself: "I am ever happy and joyful and make others also happy and joyful. I am full of educative humor. I radiate joy through humor. I respect all . . . I always

84

speak sweetly . . . I do meditation while walking and while at work also. I am a Kevala-Advaita Vedantin. I am not at all a dry-lip Vedantin . . . I do mental prostration to asses, dogs, trees, bricks, stones and all creatures."

Next day moved to Swarg Ashram. Twelve-hour free rowboat service daily. The manager gave us two totally empty rooms in a long veranda'd row building, brick and concrete. A niche and iron hooks set in the wall. A barred and shuttered window. We borrowed some straw mats to spread sleeping bags on, ran a line from hook to hook for a clothesline, put some flowers in the niche, and carried a bucket of water from the public faucet outside. After "Pure Ghee" vegetarian Brahman restaurant lunch, walked through scrub jungle and cow pastures to the river's edge, a cove of fine white sand. Finally a Ganges bath, after shying off the coffee-look of it at Patna and Banaras. Here the water is clear and cold. We washed, and washed out all our clothes—hair—glasses, cook-kit, spread them out on boulders and climbed up on a rock ourselves to wait for all to dry.

Upriver near a foot-traveler suspension bridge, three Shaivite sadhus sitting under trees, with a deformed cow and a collection box. Matted hair and long beards, on leopard hides; ash-dusted skin giving the blue sheen of Shiva who drank the world's poison and turned color. In devotional color prints he is sitting coiled with cobras, a waterpot and trident, high in mythical mountains, with his sexy bosomy wife and elephant-headed child. "Posters for the Himalaya," a fellow called those sadhus later

Swarg Ashram:

"Anna-Kshetra (A Free Kitchen):—here free food is given to Saints, Mahatmas, and the poor every day twice, in the morning and evening.

"It is a great Punya-Karma to have mango trees planted in this sacred Himalayan region . . . Up to this time several thousands of mango trees have been planted and the fruits are free to all."

March third went hunting on the hill for rishis and found a

beautiful curly-haired nineteen-year-old looking man in an orange robe who spoke English. Prem Varni, a child yogin in a swing hung from a tall pink-flowering tree over a bank, banana plants thronging up from below. "Hatha-yoga is my play, raja-yoga my meditation."

Allen said a poem for him, so he sat with closed eyes to make up one in return:

> "In our eternal journey
> In the path of infinity
> Will shine the mercy of God
> Giver of freedom and forgiveness
> I can see my . . . heart
> But he's only my real lover . . ."

Allen: "And I will worship him by eating bananas!"

Varni looked surprised and quit making his poem. He invited us to have an Astral Lunch with him, which turned out to be nothing. Enough. Back down to the river and across for an afternoon special demonstration by Shivananda's yoga instructor, a youngish man with long hair and beard named Shivalingam (Phallus of Shiva). On the roof of Mt. Kailash two hours watching and trying a number of postures including eye-rolling and mouth-grinding. Dusk.

At the riverbank a rowboat coming in, an English girl in a white sari waiting too—a drunk Nepali-looking hillboy led down by his two comrades to the water's edge. Monkeys howl in the forests. A bonfire well up the mountain. Tomorrow is Shiva's Night and the beginning day of the Kumbh Mela.

4 March, breakfast of cold puris and honey. Gusts of chilly rain. We cross the river and set out for Hardwar and the Kumbh Mela, festival of the Pitcher. Every twelve years held in Hardwar town, to celebrate the drop of immortal nectar that spilled here (by the Ganges) from a pitcher while the Surs and Asurs fought. It lasts two months and is attended by millions. Jupiter in Aquarius. 21 March, full moon; 2 April, 4 April, 13 April, the last day.

86

Busride to Hardwar through jungle and open acres of recently logged ground. Nomad camps with ponies under trees. Pass through a cholera checkpoint at the Satyanaraian Forest Guard Camp. Everyone without his paper gets a shot right there. In the past, cholera fanned out over India in the wake of pilgrims from the Kumbh.

The bus stops at the edge of town, no wheels, walk in. Crowds. Curdsellers with clay bowls tilted forward—heaters of hot dudh pouring it back and forth between brass pots. Dust whirls and whips along the ground, blowing down awnings and getting into the curds.

The opening parade:

Naga-sadhus march through town: the naked ascetics. A caparisoned elephant led by a stout muscular stark naked bearded man swinging a sword and dancing-hopping; body blue with ashes. In quintuple or triple rows another two hundred or so—all ages—most with long hair and beards, carrying conch-horns and tridents.

Mean and arrogant, padding along in the soft rain—chanting together in a low voice, all stopping and then starting—sardonic sidewise glances and the heavy insolent swing of their blue genitals like weapons.

A sudden sense of archaic tradition. Not just two or three thousand years, but fifty thousand years. A tribe of bushman shamans on the move. Or marching up out of some Pleistocene stratum under the hills.

A long line of limpy woman ascetics in ocher robes with shaved heads—old women supporting each other and singing a whimpery song. In front of the police station rows of turbaned soldiers with bayoneted rifles at attention as they pass.

The Ganges takes up the evil of all who bathe; the Naga-sadhus keep the river clean. On Kumbh day they must enter first and whoever tries to precede them will be speared. Several thousand watching as they splash, drink, and leave—putting on new ashes right away. Cool English-english speaking army officer with handie-talkie set keeping an eye on it all. His men are here and there.

Peter takes a nap under a bridge alongside peasants and pilgrims while Allen and I cogitate on the nature of nakedness. We'd thought of this approach ourselves once.

Back at Rishikesh shopping: sugar, salt, bananas, melon, oranges (mangoes not in season yet) and pineapple. Hearing the afternoon meal-bell of a local institution which supports holymen, followed a line of yellow-clad or loincloth-clad (the truly naked ones usually hang out deeper in the hills) men that appeared from nooks along the riverbanks and groves, through alleys and lanes to a ramshackle brick structure, into its courtyard, where rice was served out of one and vegetable curry out of another cauldron into the tiffin-carriers swung along by each saint or mahatma.

From Shivananda's jetty crossing the river, rains broke on us. Hid out under the edge of a ghat on the Swarg side 'til it let up some, slipped home, buying a quart of curds along the way at the Pure Ghee restaurant. Made a monster fruit-and-curds salad mixed in a two-foot terra-cotta bowl—pleasing secret hungers, all we could eat—and tea on a tiny alcohol stove in a Mountain Infantry cookpot. Thunder and lightning played on the hills and rain burst down. Shiva's Night. Banging far-off doors in the dark.

Another day climbed the jungly hill up back of Swarg, losing the trail twice and scaring a band of monkeys. Near the top came out on terraced little barley farms, the hill people with Nepal-type trousers. From the ridge could see far off the white ranges of Gangotri-Kedarnath, possibly Trisul, in the Great Himalaya.

Five natural caves in a ravine each inhabited by sadhus. Sign in front of one: "Swami Mahavir Tat Wale Baba Hours 10-1, 2-5." Farthest cave up was nicely fixed with walls built out and rustic arty touches. Pleasant old fellow a former college professor speaking a slow but elegant English. He had made the ancient choice of spending old age in the woods.

That same day packed our packs and left a contribution with the Swarg, getting in return a small brass screwtop pot containing Ganges water from the Source. It slowly leaked out in my rucksack through Almora and the Punjab, and was empty by Bombay.

'62

BUDDHISM AND THE
COMING REVOLUTION

Buddhism holds that the universe and all creatures in it are intrinsically in a state of complete wisdom, love and compassion; acting in natural response and mutual interdependence. The personal realization of this from-the-beginning state cannot be had for and by one-"self"——because it is not fully realized unless one has given the self up; and away.

In the Buddhist view, that which obstructs the effortless manifestation of this is Ignorance, which projects into fear and needless craving. Historically, Buddhist philosophers have failed to analyze out the degree to which ignorance and suffering are caused or encouraged by social factors, considering fear-and-desire to be given facts of the human condition. Consequently the major concern of Buddhist philosophy is epistemology and "psychology" with no attention paid to historical or sociological problems. Although Mahayana Buddhism has a grand vision of universal salvation, the *actual* achievement of Buddhism has been the development of practical systems of meditation toward the end of liberating a few dedicated individuals from psychological hangups and cultural conditionings. Institutional Buddhism has been conspicuously ready to accept or ignore the inequalities and tyrannies of whatever political system it found itself under. This can be death to Buddhism, because it is death to any meaningful function of compassion. Wisdom without compassion feels no pain.

No one today can afford to be innocent, or indulge himself in ignorance of the nature of contemporary governments, politics and social orders. The national polities of the modern world

90

maintain their existence by deliberately fostered craving and fear: monstrous protection rackets. The "free world" has become economically dependent on a fantastic system of stimulation of greed which cannot be fulfilled, sexual desire which cannot be satiated and hatred which has no outlet except against oneself, the persons one is supposed to love, or the revolutionary aspirations of pitiful, poverty-stricken marginal societies like Cuba or Vietnam. The conditions of the Cold War have turned all modern societies—Communist included—into vicious distorters of man's true potential. They create populations of "preta"—hungry ghosts, with giant appetites and throats no bigger than needles. The soil, the forests and all animal life are being consumed by these cancerous collectivities; the air and water of the planet is being fouled by them.

There is nothing in human nature or the requirements of human social organization which intrinsically requires that a culture be contradictory, repressive and productive of violent and frustrated personalities. Recent findings in anthropology and psychology make this more and more evident. One can prove it for himself by taking a good look at his own nature through meditation. Once a person has this much faith and insight, he must be led to a deep concern with the need for radical social change through a variety of hopefully non-violent means.

The joyous and voluntary poverty of Buddhism becomes a positive force. The traditional harmlessness and refusal to take life in any form has nation-shaking implications. The practice of meditation, for which one needs only "the ground beneath one's feet" wipes out mountains of junk being pumped into the mind by the mass media and supermarket universities. The belief in a serene and generous fulfilment of natural loving desires destroys ideologies which blind, maim and repress—and points the way to a kind of community which would amaze "moralists" and transform armies of men who are fighters because they cannot be lovers.

Avataṃsaka (Kegon) Buddhist philosophy sees the world as

a vast interrelated network in which all objects and creatures are necessary and illuminated. From one standpoint, governments, wars, or all that we consider "evil" are uncompromisingly contained in this totalistic realm. The hawk, the swoop and the hare are one. From the "human" standpoint we cannot live in those terms unless all beings see with the same enlightened eye. The Bodhisattva lives by the sufferer's standard, and he must be effective in aiding those who suffer.

The mercy of the West has been social revolution; the mercy of the East has been individual insight into the basic self/void. We need both. They are both contained in the traditional three aspects of the Dharma path: wisdom (prajña), meditation (dhyāna), and morality (śīla). Wisdom is intuitive knowledge of the mind of love and clarity that lies beneath one's ego-driven anxieties and aggressions. Meditation is going into the mind to see this for yourself—over and over again, until it becomes the mind you live in. Morality is bringing it back out in the way you live, through personal example and responsible action, ultimately toward the true community (saṇgha) of "all beings." This last aspect means, for me, supporting any cultural and economic revolution that moves clearly toward a free, international, classless world. It means using such means as civil disobedience, outspoken criticism, protest, pacifism, voluntary poverty and even gentle violence if it comes to a matter of restraining some impetuous redneck. It means affirming the widest possible spectrum of non-harmful individual behavior —defending the right of individuals to smoke hemp, eat peyote, be polygynous, polyandrous or homosexual. Worlds of behavior and custom long banned by the Judaeo-Capitalist-Christian-Marxist West. It means respecting intelligence and learning, but not as greed or means to personal power. Working on one's own responsibility, but willing to work with a group. "Forming the new society within the shell of the old"—the I.W.W. slogan of fifty years ago.

The traditional cultures are in any case doomed, and rather than cling to their good aspects hopelessly it should be remembered that whatever is or ever was in any other culture can be reconstructed from the unconscious, through meditation. In fact, it is my own view that the coming revolution will close the circle and link us in many ways with the most creative aspects of our archaic past. If we are lucky we may eventually arrive at a totally integrated world culture with matrilineal descent, free-form marriage, natural-credit communist economy, less industry, far less population and lots more national parks.

GLACIER PEAK
WILDERNESS AREA

1: IX: 65   N. Fork Sauk Road to Sunup Lake

Bingley Gap about 4500′. Trail fork old Pugh Creek,
Whitechuck trails—all overgrown. Round Lake is another
two miles over the ridge and a good ways down. No place
to camp along the way. Sunup Lake—I'd come to think Round
and Sunup were the same lake—is another ¾ mile beyond
—wouldn't have known where, if it hadn't been for two
Geological Survey men we ran onto, up here surveying the
trail a bit for the 1/24,000 sheet to come out in another two
years. They explained it was above the trail three hundred feet,
totally unmarked. I went up there—no place to camp. A
good site right by the trail on the outlet creek from Sunup, though.
Clouds cleared off at sunset. But in the middle of the night,
came down again.

"Come straight up the forty-eight switchback
     mountain trail!" koan. Plod, plod, thump thump,
chasing my sierra cup a bit down the slope—and rapping with
Justine that pleasure isn't as simple as some folks think—
to heave and sweat and strain (ah, forcing to the edge of limits,
of endurance) makes a kind of pleasure.

Nō play *Yamauba*—forever walking over mountains; over
mountains—red leaves falling—striking through winter
snowstorms—spring sticky alder buds—summer bees. J. sees
me wandering way off ahead. And when she catches up says,

"You're already spoken for. . . . you belong to the mountains"—
no human man can belong to the mountains except as they
are nature, and nature is woman.

2:IX   Sunup Lake to Lake Byrne

   Cloudy and foggy, with occasional breaks of sun. Sloan
mountain and Bedal mountain

               not   to   be   seen.

   Leave 9.30. Trail obscure through meadows. Mistake
a pond below for "Hardtack Lake"—arrive at True Hardtack
2.30 p.m.

               descending to a previous pond for
            lunch over steep heather
pick your way thru like a beast

Justine strips down and washes breasts and arms, tho all
is chill; her jeans color of the lakeside sedge and hillside
heather, hair the color of the mountain wind.

            [Pugh creek goes into the Whitechuck
               the Whitechuck goes into the Sauk
                  the Sauk goes into the Skagit
                     the Skagit goes into the Sound.]

Rats, lambs, men, and whales
                              all drink milk.


```
┌─────────────────────────────────────┐
│                                      │
│      North  Fork  Sauk  Trail        │
│                                      │
│      White Mt Shelter    5 →         │
│      White Pass          9 →         │
│                                      │
└─────────────────────────────────────┘
```


95

3: IX   Lake Byrne down to Kennedy Hotsprings

Cold mountain, Cold mountain.   —from Hardtack Lake
to Lake Byrne, two miles, it took us two hours. Chill wind and
mist—"Mist people, GO AWAY!" Camp, set up tent and
ditch it; big fire; but no rains in the night. Allen's *Om*. All that
Allen really misses is the view.

Sitting around the fire in the cloudy mountains shivering
and hovering, writing down and talking, all about our dreams.

Up on the ridge south of the lake, looking to Black Mountain
—up high, skyline, tiny white things which resolved at length
into three adult mountain goats and one kid. Ambling slowly
along a face, above the snow. Mountain goat trails, with bits of
white wool clinging on the Mountain Hemlock and Alpine Fir
—right down to here.

Going along the trail traveling HIGH. Step, step, flying
paces like Tibetans—strangely familiar massive vistas—the trail
is *Right*. All the different figures one becomes—old Japanese
woodcutter; exiled traveler in a Chinese scroll—

Allen and Justine somewhere behind, chant

> *Hari   Om   Namo   Shiva*

A party of fishermen—two men, a woman and a child,
struggling up trail come on us then. Allen looks on
them graciously and explains, "WE are *forest beatniks*."

Kennedy hotsprings—a rough axe-made cedar footbridge.
Guard Station. Went to talk, the Guard's wife was on
Sourdough Mt. Lookout for four years during the forties.

And the springs, ten yards off the little Whitechuck river,
orange or saffron deposits downslope from it, the mineral
drainage—a deep square well of bubbling yellow hot water lined
with cedar logs—just right, heat of a Japanese public bath,
we all get in and float, look up, from the darkest V-crack
bottom of a high mountain valley, the open sky clouds behind
Douglas Fir limbs, Rushy Murky bowel water of Geology Gods
flowing up between our toes—embracing Justine, lightly

drifting in the water, holding her down at her center, her eyes
closed, ragged limbs and gray sky far above.

       sitting on the rocks watching fog roll
       cold mountains, cold mountains
mountain goats white
specks across the valley

  Justine's red towel turban, glowing face, walking back to
make dinner, home's a smoky shady log shelter—safe and
warm. But for a mouse
      that longed for human hair.

4:IX   Kennedy Hotsprings to White Pass

> **Whitechuck Trail**
>
> ← White Pass   10
> ← Cascade Crest Tr   2

> **Cascade Crest Trail**
>
> Indian Pass   13 →
> White Pass   7 →
> ← Milk Creek Pass   9

Thick moss on slide-boulders. Ripe huckleberries.

      sun patches in the gorge
         whitechuck river
     white foam falls,
     thru the tops of spruce and hemlock

       white sailing clouds.
   the brilliance of *black*.

September mountains,
ripe huckleberries
        a few elderly mosquitoes with
        chilly wings.

5:IX   at White Pass camp

Today checking out route to Whitechuck Glacier

White Pass

Indian Pass   3 →
White River and Indian
River Trails   →
Blue Lake Way   5 →

Anvil notch to White Pass backsight: azimuth 193°
Anvil notch to basin;   azimuth 35°
& it takes about 45 minutes from Anvil notch to White
Pass.
        J., with blistered feet, stays in the camp on the
edge of the cliff, sheltering in a clump of Mountain Hemlock, all
day—while Allen and I run the ridge and look a bit at
Glacier Peak and Whitechuck Glacier.
        Monte Cristo range a jagged wall out west.

6: IX   Glacier Peak Ascent

    Up at 4 a.m. cold müesli—mountain mush—perfect
bright star night.   *Orion Rising*
        —now that's more like what it really means.

                —GOING—

First Stage.

   Up the grassy slope above the shelter, and then right back
down to camp—Justine nested in all the sleeping bags—
to get the forgotten goldline rope. Allen's cigarette glowing in the
dark. A yodel from the top of the ridge.

Second Stage.

   Along sidehill trail in the dark—not even using flashlight—
the first cliffs, the second cliffs, the duck. Up to anvil
notch. Hard snow.

Third Stage.

   Grassy trail to the top of a snowfield; down the steep loose
scree alongside and across at a narrow neck—down a short
ridge and under another field—then angle below some rocks to
the bottom of the moraine valley. Creeks frozen under the
snow. Shat.

Fourth Stage.

   Up the moraine basin picking way through boulders and
walking on frozen mud. Ice on ponds. Rise and rise, but still
no glacier. Getting light; Rainier and Baker seen now,
gathering pre-sun glow. Down slight to the edge of the
Whitechuck Glacier.

Fifth Stage.

   Rope up on glacier. Frozen and crystal; rough—no need
for crampons, no need for rope, in fact. Below perpendicular
rock walls like Karakorum photos taken on the Duke of
Abruzzi's expedition. At the NE end snow leading back up on
the ridge. Up that on rock along the side, the crest between
Whitechuck and Suiattle Glacier. Full sunrise on us now.

Needs must descend some snow—two small rock patches, climb again to reach the pumice ridge, a saddle, a cairn I built even higher to become a chorten.

Sixth Stage.

A piece of silver rotten wood found by the cairn—faint carved indentation, it reads "Bakos Pass". And a pond a bit below, lying under a snowfield and against the talus. Went down to drink. Iced over—breaking it, and slide the broken pieces down the sheet of ice, tinkling, silently slipping off into other open water.

Ridges and ridges, out the Suiattle River valley. Up the pumice ridge, which turns to talus. Cogitating routes—a lower or upper notch across the Chocolate Glacier.

Seventh Stage.

Rope up again, at the edge of ice and rock. Beside the skeleton of a mountain goat—clear up here—some skin still clinging. Somebody took the horns. Contouring eastward up the glacier, only a few crevasses; rocks rattling down the cliffs of the false summit above. To the icefalls. Sheets of water running underfoot, beneath the snow and on the ice. Chop a basin with the iceaxe, let it fill and drink. After two false starts, find a good way through the icefalls, climbing big tumbled blocks.

Eighth Stage.

"Left to the col." The upper glacier full of wide crevasses—crossing bridges to a higher lip. Between two huge ones—both of us exposed. Around, feeling through; Allen Ginsberg handling my rope and poised for a belay; and toward the top of the icebridge a bee that buzzed and buzzed around. Me some kind of meat flower.

100

Ninth Stage.

A flock of birds, all cheeping and flying over the edge
from void to void. Pumice again. Crampons off and start
up tiring slidy rock. An hour and a half to the top.
Mazama box chained to a rock—a snowy crest—mountains
around, around, around, around. I laughed and laughed. Allen
was still coming up, a ways below.

Ross Petrie climbed it just the day before, from the other
side, with a group from Portland. Nice to know he's still
climbing. To see his name in his hand in the summit book.

So many mountains, on so clear a day, the mind is
staggered, and so looks to little things like pilot bread and
cheese and bits of dried fruit. From Canada to
Oregon, and ranges both east and west—the blue mass
of the Olympics far over hazy Puget Sound—"You mean
there's a Senator for all this?"

—COMING BACK—

Run down the pumice to the col.

Rope up and weave between crevasses, long strides
down the glaciers. Sparrows on snow pecking wind-blown
seeds? A jet *below* us, hissing up the Whitechuck valley.

Slipping and sliding across the Whitechuck—slush
crystals, dirt, surface water, water underneath. A huge
vaginal cave visible down on the Suiattle.

Step in the melted mud up to boot tops.

Across the moraine—green and full of moss in sunlight—
pastoral and warm, compared with up above—

Climb back to the anvil. Late sun, deep greens. On
the ridges. Yodel from the crest and pound and march,
along the side to White Pass, and shelter a bit below, the
stovepipe smoking. Justine in the doorway. Hot bouillon from
her hands and smoky dark inside. Just sunset now and
fading light back of Monte Cristo peaks. Off weary boots.

7: IX.   White Pass

Up in a meadow on the ridge, in the sun, making love on
oatsack burlap horsefeed bags. Green, blue, white snow
patches. Dying hellebore, summer's over.
A morning bathing.   green, green, the side of
                          White Mountain
                 deep, deep, the valleys below.
Firewood chopping with a pulaski.
Shelter—inside like a primitive Japanese farmhouse.
Down trail in the afternoon, eating purple-blue huckleberries
along the way. Into valley bottom and forest shade, the White
Mountain shelter. Crosscut saws, and burned shake
nameboards overhead. Pepper, sugar, flour.

Cascade Crest Tr

← Milk Creek Pass   17½
    Dishpan Gap   7 →
    Indian Pass   4 →

8: IX: 65   White Mountain Shelter to Sloan Creek

Salal, skunk cabbage, Devil's club, Oregon grape,
maidenhair fern.
11:30 a.m. get to Sloan Creek and the logging road.
A pickup truck and some young loggers with
shortbar chainsaws—I ask them

"Why you cutting back the brush along the road?"
"—Can't get the Forest Service to do it—
    have to do it ourselves—
    so our guys won't run over each other
    trucking out the logs."

PASSAGE TO MORE
THAN INDIA

> "It will be a revival, in higher form, of the liberty,
> equality, and fraternity of the ancient gentes."
> —LEWIS HENRY MORGAN

The Tribe

The celebrated human Be-In in San Francisco, January of
1967, was called "A Gathering of the Tribes." The two
posters: one based on a photograph of a Shaivite sadhu with
his long matted hair, ashes and beard; the other based on an old
etching of a Plains Indian approaching a powwow on his horse
—the carbine that had been cradled in his left arm replaced
by a guitar. The Indians, and the Indian. The tribes
were Berkeley, North Beach, Big Sur, Marin County, Los
Angeles, and the host, Haight-Ashbury. Outriders were present
from New York, London and Amsterdam. Out on the polo field
that day the splendidly clad ab/originals often fell into clusters,
with children, a few even under banners. These were the clans.

Large old houses are rented communally by a group,
occupied by couples and singles (or whatever combinations)
and their children. In some cases, especially in the rock-and-roll
business and with light-show groups, they are all working
together on the same creative job. They might even be a legal
corporation. Some are subsistence farmers out in the
country, some are contractors and carpenters in small coast
towns. One girl can stay home and look after all the children
while the other girls hold jobs. They will all be cooking

and eating together and they may well be brown-rice vegetarians. There might not be much alcohol or tobacco around the house, but there will certainly be a stash of marijuana and probably some LSD. If the group has been together for some time it may be known by some informal name, magical and natural. These house-holds provide centers in the city and also out in the country for loners and rangers; gathering places for the scattered smaller hip families and havens for the questing adolescent children of the neighborhood. The clan sachems will sometimes gather to talk about larger issues—police or sheriff department harassments, busts, anti-Vietnam projects, dances and gatherings.

All this is known fact. The number of committed total tribesmen is not so great, but there is a large population of crypto-members who move through many walks of life undetected and only put on their beads and feathers for special occasions. Some are in the academies, others in the legal or psychiatric professions—very useful friends indeed. The number of people who use marijuana regularly and have experienced LSD is (considering it's all illegal) staggering. The impact of all this on the cultural and imaginative life of the nation—even the politics—is enormous.

And yet, there's nothing very new about it, in spite of young hippies just in from the suburbs for whom the "beat generation" is a kalpa away. For several centuries now Western Man has been ponderously preparing himself for a new look at the inner world and the spiritual realms. Even in the centers of nineteenth-century materialism there were dedicated seekers—some within Christianity, some in the arts, some within the occult circles. Witness William Butler Yeats. My own opinion is that we are now experiencing a surfacing (in a specifically "American" incarnation) of the Great Subculture which goes back as far perhaps as the late Paleolithic.

This subculture of illuminati has been a powerful

undercurrent in all higher civilizations. In China it manifested as Taoism, not only Lao-tzu but the later Yellow Turban revolt and medieval Taoist secret societies; and the Zen Buddhists up till early Sung. Within Islam the Sufis; in India the various threads converged to produce Tantrism. In the West it has been represented largely by a string of heresies starting with the Gnostics, and on the folk level by "witchcraft."

Buddhist Tantrism, or Vajrayana as it's also known, is probably the finest and most modern statement of this ancient shamanistic-yogic-gnostic-socioeconomic view: that mankind's mother is Nature and Nature should be tenderly respected; that man's life and destiny is growth and enlightenment in self-disciplined freedom; that the divine has been made flesh and that flesh is divine; that we not only should but *do* love one another. This view has been harshly suppressed in the past as threatening to both Church and State. Today, on the contrary, these values seem almost biologically essential to the survival of humanity.

The Family

Lewis Henry Morgan (d. 1881) was a New York lawyer. He was asked by his club to reorganize it "after the pattern of the Iroquois confederacy." His research converted him into a defender of tribal rights and started him on his career as an amateur anthropologist. His major contribution was a broad theory of social evolution which is still useful. Morgan's *Ancient Society* inspired Engels to write *Origins of the Family, Private Property and the State* (1884, and still in print in both Russia and China), in which the relations between the rights of women, sexuality and the family, and attitudes toward property and power are tentatively explored. The pivot is the revolutionary implications of the custom of matrilineal descent, which Engels learned from Morgan; the Iroquois are matrilineal.

A schematic history of the family:

Hunters and gatherers—a loose monogamy within communal clans usually reckoning descent in the female line, i.e., matrilineal.

Early agriculturalists—a tendency toward group and polyandrous marriage, continued matrilineal descent and smaller-sized clans.

Pastoral nomads—a tendency toward stricter monogamy and patrilineal descent; but much premarital sexual freedom.

Iron-Age agriculturalists—property begins to accumulate and the family system changes to monogamy or polygyny with patrilineal descent. Concern with the legitimacy of heirs.

Civilization so far has implied a patriarchal, patrilineal family. Any other system allows too much creative sexual energy to be released into channels which are "unproductive." In the West, the clan, or gens, disappeared gradually, and social organization was ultimately replaced by political organization, within which separate male-oriented families compete: the modern state.

Engels' Marxian classic implies that the revolution cannot be completely achieved in merely political terms. Monogamy and patrilineal descent may well be great obstructions to the inner changes required for a people to truly live by "communism." Marxists after Engels let these questions lie. Russia and China today are among the world's staunchest supporters of monogamous, sexually turned-off families. Yet Engels' insights were not entirely ignored. The Anarcho-Syndicalists showed a sense for experimental social reorganization. American anarchists and the I.W.W. lived a kind of communalism, with some lovely stories handed down of free love—their slogan was more than just words: "Forming the new society within the shell of the old." San Francisco poets and gurus were attending meetings of the "Anarchist Circle"—old Italians and Finns— in the 1940's.

In many American Indian cultures it is obligatory for every member to get out of the society, out of the human nexus, and "out of his head," at least once in his life. He returns from his solitary vision quest with a secret name, a protective animal spirit, a secret song. It is his "power." The culture honors the man who has visited other realms.

Peyote, the mushroom, morning-glory seeds and Jimson-weed are some of the best-known herbal aids used by Indian cultures to assist in the quest. Most tribes apparently achieved these results simply through yogic-type disciplines: including sweat-baths, hours of dancing, fasting and total isolation. After the decline of the apocalyptic fervor of Wovoka's Ghost Dance religion (a pan-Indian movement of the 1880's and 1890's which believed that if all the Indians would dance the Ghost Dance with their Ghost shirts on, the Buffalo would rise from the ground, trample the white men to death in their dreams, and all the dead game would return; America would be restored to the Indians), the peyote cult spread and established itself in most of the western American tribes. Although the peyote religion conflicts with pre-existing tribal religions in a few cases (notably with the Pueblo), there is no doubt that the cult has been a positive force, helping the Indians maintain a reverence for their traditions and land through their period of greatest weakness—which is now over. European scholars were investigating peyote in the twenties. It is even rumored that Dr. Carl Jung was experimenting with peyote then. A small band of white peyote users emerged, and peyote was easily available in San Francisco by the late 1940's. In Europe some researchers on these alkaloid compounds were beginning to synthesize them. There is a karmic connection between the peyote cult of the Indians and the discovery of lysergic acid in Switzerland.

Peyote and acid have a curious way of tuning some people in

to the local soil. The strains and stresses deep beneath one
in the rock, the flow and fabric of wildlife around, the
human history of Indians on this continent. Older powers
become evident: west of the Rockies, the ancient creator-trickster,
Coyote. Jaime de Angulo, a now-legendary departed Spanish
shaman and anthropologist, was an authentic Coyote-medium.
One of the most relevant poetry magazines is called *Coyote's
Journal*. For many, the invisible presence of the Indian, and the
heartbreaking beauty of America work without fasting or herbs.
We make these contacts simply by walking the Sierra or
Mohave, learning the old edibles, singing and watching.

The Jewel in the Lotus

At the Congress of World Religions in Chicago in the 1890's,
two of the most striking figures were Swami Vivekananda
(Shri Ramakrishna's disciples) and Shaku Soyen, the
Zen Master and Abbot of Engaku-ji, representing Japanese
Rinzai Zen. Shaku Soyen's interpreter was a college
student named Teitaro Suzuki. The Ramakrishna-Vivekananda
line produced scores of books and established Vedanta
centers all through the Western world. A small band of Zen
monks under Shaku Sokatsu (disciple of Shaku Soyen) was
raising strawberries in Hayward, California, in 1907. Shigetsu
Sasaki, later to be known as the Zen Master Sokei-an, was
roaming the timberlands of the Pacific Northwest just
before World War I, and living on a Puget Sound Island
with Indians for neighbors. D. T. Suzuki's books are to be
found today in the libraries of biochemists and on stone ledges
under laurel trees in the open-air camps of Big Sur gypsies.
    A Californian named Walter Y. Evans-Wentz, who sensed
that the mountains on his family's vast grazing lands really
did have spirits in them, went to Oxford to study the Celtic belief
in fairies and then to Sikkim to study Vajrayana under a
lama. His best-known book is *The Tibetan Book of the Dead*.
    Those who do not have the money or time to go to India

or Japan, but who think a great deal about the wisdom traditions, have remarkable results when they take LSD. The *Bhagavad-Gita,* the Hindu mythologies, *The Serpent Power,* the *Laṅkavatara-sūtra,* the *Upanishads,* the *Hevajra-tantra,* the *Mahanirvana-tantra*—to name a few texts—become, they say, finally clear to them. They often feel they must radically reorganize their lives to harmonize with such insights.

In several American cities traditional meditation halls of both Rinzai and Soto Zen are flourishing. Many of the newcomers turned to traditional meditation after initial acid experience. The two types of experience seem to inform each other.

The Heretics

> "When Adam delved and Eve span,
> Who was then a gentleman?"

The memories of a Golden Age—the Garden of Eden—the Age of the Yellow Ancestor—were genuine expressions of civilization and its discontents. Harking back to societies where women and men were more free with each other; where there was more singing and dancing; where there were no serfs and priests and kings.

Projected into future time in Christian culture, this dream of the Millennium became the soil of many heresies. It is a dream handed down right to our own time—of ecological balance, classless society, social and economic freedom. It is actually one of the possible futures open to us. To those who stubbornly argue "it's against human nature," we can only patiently reply that you must know your own nature before you can say this. Those who have gone into their own natures deeply have, for several thousand years now, been reporting that we have nothing to fear if we are willing to train ourselves, to open up, explore and grow.

One of the most significant medieval heresies was the Brotherhood of the Free Spirit, of which Hieronymus Bosch was probably a member. The Brotherhood believed that God was immanent in everything, and that once one had experienced this God-presence in himself he became a Free Spirit; he was again living in the Garden of Eden. The brothers and sisters held their meetings naked, and practiced much sharing. They "confounded clerics with the subtlety of their arguments." It was complained that "they have no uniform . . . sometimes they dress in a costly and dissolute fashion, sometimes most miserably, all according to time and place." The Free Spirits had communal houses in secret all through Germany and the Lowlands, and wandered freely among them. Their main supporters were the well-organized and affluent weavers.

When brought before the Inquisition they were not charged with witchcraft, but with believing that man was divine, and with making love too freely, with orgies. Thousands were burned. There are some who have as much hostility to the adepts of the subculture today. This may be caused not so much by the outlandish clothes and dope, as by the nutty insistence on "love." The West and Christian culture on one level deeply wants love to win—and having decided (after several sad tries) that love can't, people who still say it will are like ghosts from an old dream.

Love begins with the family and its network of erotic and responsible relationships. A slight alteration of family structure will project a different love-and-property outlook through a whole culture . . . thus the communism and free love of the Christian heresies. This is a real razor's edge. Shall the lion lie down with the lamb? And make love even? The Garden of Eden.

White Indians

The modern American family is the smallest and most barren family that has ever existed. Each newly-married couple

110

moves to a new house or apartment—no uncles or grandmothers come to live with them. There are seldom more than two or three children. The children live with their peers and leave home early. Many have never had the least sense of family.

I remember sitting down to Christmas dinner eighteen years ago in a communal house in Portland, Oregon, with about twelve others my own age, all of whom had no place they wished to go home to. That house was my first discovery of harmony and community with fellow beings. This has been the experience of hundreds of thousands of men and women all over America since the end of World War II. Hence the talk about the growth of a "new society." But more; these gatherings have been people spending time with each other—talking, delving, making love. Because of the sheer amount of time "wasted" together (without TV) they know each other better than most Americans know their own family. Add to this the mind-opening and personality-revealing effects of grass and acid, and it becomes possible to predict the emergence of groups who live by mutual illumination—have seen themselves as of one mind and one flesh—the "single eye" of the heretical English Ranters; the meaning of sahajiya, "born together"—the name of the latest flower of the Tantric community tradition in Bengal.

Industrial society indeed appears to be finished. Many of us are, again, hunters and gatherers. Poets, musicians, nomadic engineers and scholars; fact-diggers, searchers and re-searchers scoring in rich foundation territory. Horse-traders in lore and magic. The super hunting-bands of mercenaries like Rand or CIA may in some ways belong to the future, if they can be transformed by the ecological conscience, or acid, to which they are very vulnerable. A few of us are literally hunters and gatherers, playfully studying the old techniques of acorn flour, seaweed-gathering, yucca-fiber, rabbit snaring and bow hunting. The densest Indian population in pre-Columbian America north of Mexico was in Marin, Sonoma and Napa Counties, California.

And finally, to go back to Morgan and Engels, sexual mores

111

and the family are changing in the same direction. Rather than the "breakdown of the family" we should see this as the transition to a new form of family. In the near future, I think it likely that the freedom of women and the tribal spirit will make it possible for us to formalize our marriage relationships in any way we please—as groups, or polygynously or polyandrously, as well as monogamously. I use the word "formalize" only in the sense of make public and open the relationships, and to sacramentalize them; to see family as part of the divine ecology. Because it is simpler, more natural, and breaks up tendencies toward property accumulation by individual families, matrilineal descent seems ultimately indicated. Such families already exist. Their children are different in personality structure and outlook from anybody in the history of Western culture since the destruction of Knossos.

The American Indian is the vengeful ghost lurking in the back of the troubled American mind. Which is why we lash out with such ferocity and passion, so muddied a heart, at the black-haired young peasants and soldiers who are the "Viet Cong." That ghost will claim the next generation as its own. When this has happened, citizens of the USA will at last begin to be Americans, truly at home on the continent, in love with their land. The chorus of a Cheyenne Indian Ghost dance song —"hi-niswa' vita'ki'ni"—"We shall live again."

> "Passage to more than India!
> Are thy wings plumed indeed for such far flights?
> O soul, voyagest thou indeed on voyages like those?"

WHY TRIBE

We use the term Tribe because it suggests the type of new society now emerging within the industrial nations. In America of course the word has associations with the American Indians, which we like. This new subculture is in fact more similar to that ancient and successful tribe, the European Gypsies—a group without nation or territory which maintains its own values, its language and religion, no matter what country it may be in.

The Tribe proposes a totally different style: based on community houses, villages and ashrams; tribe-run farms or workshops or companies; large open families; pilgrimages and wanderings from center to center. A synthesis of Gandhian "village anarchism" and I.W.W. syndicalism. Interesting visionary pamphlets along these lines were written several years ago by Gandhians Richard Gregg and Appa Patwardhan. The Tribe proposes personal responsibilities rather than abstract centralized government, taxes and advertising-agency-plus-Mafia type international brainwashing corporations.

In the United States and Europe the Tribe has evolved gradually over the last fifty years—since the end of World War I —in response to the increasing insanity of the modern nations. As the number of alienated intellectuals, creative types and general social misfits grew, they came to recognize each other by various minute signals. Much of this energy was channeled into Communism in the thirties and early forties. All the anarchists and left-deviationists—and many Trotskyites—were tribesmen at heart. After World War II, another generation looked at Communist rhetoric with a fresh eye and saw that within the Communist governments (and states of mind) there are too many of the same things as are wrong with "capitalism" —too much anger and murder. The suspicion grew that perhaps the whole Western Tradition, of which Marxism is but a (Millennial Protestant) part, is off the track. This led many people to study other major civilizations—India and China— to see what they could learn.

It's an easy step from the dialectic of Marx and Hegel to an interest in the dialectic of early Taoism, the *I Ching,* and the yin-yang theories. From Taoism it is another easy step to the philosophies and mythologies of India—vast, touching the deepest areas of the mind, and with a view of the ultimate nature of the universe which is almost identical with the most sophisticated thought in modern physics—that truth, whatever it is, which is called "The Dharma."

Next comes a concern with deepening one's understanding in an experiential way: abstract philosophical understanding is simply not enough. At this point many, myself included, found in the Buddha-Dharma a practical method for clearing one's mind of the trivia, prejudices and false values that our conditioning had laid on us—and more important, an approach to the basic problem of how to penetrate to the deepest non-self Self. Today we have many who are exploring the Ways of Zen, Vajrayāna, Yoga, Shamanism, Psychedelics. The Buddha-Dharma is a long, gentle, human dialog—2,500 years of quiet conversation—on the nature of human nature and the eternal Dharma—and practical methods of realization.

In the course of these studies it became evident that the "truth" in Buddhism and Hinduism is not dependent in any sense on Indian or Chinese culture; and that "India" and "China"—as societies—are as burdensome to human beings as any others; perhaps more so. It became clear that "Hinduism" and "Buddhism" as social institutions had long been accomplices of the State in burdening and binding people, rather than serving to liberate them. Just like the other Great Religions.

At this point, looking once more quite closely at history both East and West, some of us noticed the similarities in certain

114

small but influential heretical and esoteric movements. These schools of thought and practice were usually suppressed, or diluted and made harmless, in whatever society they appeared. Peasant witchcraft in Europe, Tantrism in Bengal, Quakers in England, Tachikawa-ryū in Japan, Ch'an in China. These are all outcroppings of the Great Subculture which runs underground all through history. This is the tradition that runs without break from Paleo-Siberian Shamanism and Magdalenian cave-painting; through megaliths and Mysteries, astronomers, ritualists, alchemists and Albigensians; gnostics and vagantes, right down to Golden Gate Park.

The Great Subculture has been attached in part to the official religions but is different in that it transmits a community style of life, with an ecstatically positive vision of spiritual and physical love; and is opposed for very fundamental reasons to the Civilization Establishment.

It has taught that man's natural being is to be trusted and followed; that we need not look to a model or rule imposed from outside in searching for the center; and that in following the grain, one is being truly "moral." It has recognized that for one to "follow the grain" it is necessary to look exhaustively into the negative and demonic potentials of the Unconscious, and by recognizing these powers—symbolically acting them out —one releases himself from these forces. By this profound exorcism and ritual drama, the Great Subculture destroys the one credible claim of Church and State to a necessary function.

All this is subversive to civilization: for civilization is built on hierarchy and specialization. A ruling class, to survive, must propose a Law: a law to work must have a hook into the social psyche—and the most effective way to achieve this is to make people doubt their natural worth and instincts, especially sexual. To make "human nature" suspect is also to make Nature—the wilderness—the adversary. Hence the ecological crisis of today.

We came, therefore, (and with many Western thinkers before us) to suspect that civilization may be overvalued. Before anyone says "This is ridiculous, we all know civilization is a necessary thing," let him read some cultural anthropology. Take a look at the lives of South African Bushmen, Micronesian navigators, the Indians of California; the researches of Claude Lévi-Strauss. Everything we have thought about man's welfare needs to be rethought. The tribe, it seems, is the newest development in the Great Subculture. We have almost unintentionally linked ourselves to a transmission of gnosis, a potential social order, and techniques of enlightenment, surviving from prehistoric times.

The most advanced developments of modern science and technology have come to support some of these views. Consequently the modern Tribesman, rather than being old-fashioned in his criticism of civilization, is the most relevant type in contemporary society. Nationalism, warfare, heavy industry and consumership, are already outdated and useless. The next great step of mankind is to step into the nature of his own mind—the real question is "just what is consciousness?"— and we must make the most intelligent and creative use of science in exploring these questions. The man of wide international experience, much learning and leisure—luxurious product of our long and sophisticated history—may with good reason wish to live simply, with few tools and minimal clothes, close to nature.

The Revolution has ceased to be an ideological concern. Instead, people are trying it out right now—communism in small communities, new family organization. A million people in America and another million in England and Europe. A vast underground in Russia, which will come out in the open four or five years hence, is now biding. How do they recognize each other? Not always by beards, long hair, bare feet or beads. The signal is a bright and tender look; calmness and gentleness, freshness and ease of manner. Men, women and children—all of whom together hope to follow the timeless path of love and wisdom, in affectionate company with the sky, winds, clouds, trees, waters, animals and grasses——this is the tribe.

POETRY AND THE PRIMITIVE

Notes on Poetry as an Ecological Survival Technique

Bilateral Symmetry

"Poetry" as the skilled and inspired use of the voice and language to embody rare and powerful states of mind that are in immediate origin personal to the singer, but at deep levels common to all who listen. "Primitive" as those societies which have remained non-literate and non-political while necessarily exploring and developing in directions that civilized societies have tended to ignore. Having fewer tools, no concern with history, a living oral tradition rather than an accumulated library, no overriding social goals, and considerable freedom of sexual and inner life, such people live vastly in the present. Their daily reality is a fabric of friends and family, the field of feeling and energy that one's own body is, the earth they stand on and the wind that wraps around it; and various areas of consciousness.

At this point some might be tempted to say that the primitive's real life is no different from anybody else's. I think this is not so. To live in the "mythological present" in close relation to nature and in basic but disciplined body/mind states suggests a wider-ranging imagination and a closer subjective knowledge of one's own physical properties than is usually available to men living (as they themselves describe it) impotently and inadequately in "history"—their mind-content programmed, and their caressing of nature complicated by the extensions and abstractions which elaborate tools are. A hand pushing a button may wield great power, but that hand will never learn what a hand can do. Unused capacities go sour.

Poetry must sing or speak from authentic experience. Of all the streams of civilized tradition with roots in the paleolithic, poetry is one of the few that can realistically claim an unchanged function and a relevance which will outlast most of the activities that surround us today. Poets, as few others, must live close to the world that primitive men are in: the world, in its nakedness, which is fundamental for all of us—birth, love, death; the sheer fact of being alive.

Music, dance, religion, and philosophy of course have archaic roots—a shared origin with poetry. Religion has tended to become the social justifier, a lackey to power, instead of the vehicle of hair-raising liberating and healing realizations. Dance has mostly lost its connection with ritual drama, the miming of animals, or tracing the maze of the spiritual journey. Most music takes too many tools. The poet can make it on his own voice and mother tongue, while steering a course between crystal clouds of utterly incommunicable non-verbal states—and the gleaming daggers and glittering nets of language.

In one school of Mahayana Buddhism, they talk about the "Three Mysteries." These are Body, Voice, and Mind. The things that are what living *is* for us, in life. Poetry is the vehicle of the mystery of voice. The universe, as they sometimes say, is a vast breathing body.

With artists, certain kinds of scientists, yogins, and poets, a kind of mind-sense is not only surviving but modestly flourishing in the twentieth century. Claude Lévi-Strauss (*The Savage Mind*) sees no problem in the continuity: ". . . it is neither the mind of savages nor that of primitive or archaic humanity, but rather mind in its untamed state as distinct from mind cultivated or domesticated for yielding a return . . . We are better able to

118

understand today that it is possible for the two to coexist and interpenetrate in the same way that (in theory at least) it is possible for natural species, of which some are in their savage state and others transformed by agriculture and domestication, to coexist and cross . . . whether one deplores or rejoices in the fact, there are still zones in which savage thought, like savage species, is relatively protected. This is the case of art, to which our civilization accords the status of a national park."

Making Love with Animals

By civilized times, hunting was a sport of kings. The early Chinese emperors had vast fenced hunting reserves; peasants were not allowed to shoot deer. Millennia of experience, the proud knowledges of hunting magic—animal habits—and the skills of wild plant and herb gathering were all but scrubbed away. Much has been said about the frontier in American history, but overlooking perhaps some key points: the American confrontation with a vast wild ecology, an earthly paradise of grass, water, and game—was mind-shaking. Americans lived next to vigorous primitives whom they could not help but respect and even envy, for three hundred years. Finally, as ordinary men supporting their families, they often hunted for food. Although marginal peasants in Europe and Asia did remain part-time hunters at the bottom of the social scale, these Americans were the vanguard of an expanding culture. For Americans, "nature" means wilderness, the untamed realm of total freedom—not brutish and nasty, but beautiful and terrible. Something is always eating at the American heart like acid: it is the knowledge of what we have done to our continent, and to the American Indian.

Other civilizations have done the same, but at a pace too slow to be remembered. One finds evidence in T'ang and Sung poetry that the barren hills of central and northern China were once richly forested. The Far Eastern love of nature has become fear of nature: gardens and pine trees are tormented and controlled. Chinese nature poets were too often retired bureaucrats living on two or three acres of trees trimmed by hired gardeners. The professional nature-aesthetes of modern Japan, tea-teachers and flower-arrangers, are amazed to hear that only a century ago dozens of species of birds passed through Kyoto where today only swallows and sparrows can be seen; and the aesthetes can scarcely distinguish those. "Wild" in the Far East means uncontrollable, objectionable, crude, sexually unrestrained, violent; actually ritually polluting. China cast off mythology, which means its own dreams, with hairy cocks and gaping pudenda, millennia ago; and modern Japanese families participating in an "economic miracle" can have daughters in college who are not sure which hole babies come out of. One of the most remarkable intuitions in Western thought was Rousseau's Noble Savage: the idea that perhaps civilization has something to learn from the primitive.

Man is a beautiful animal. We know this because other animals admire us and love us. Almost all animals are beautiful and paleolithic hunters were deeply moved by it. To hunt means to use your body and senses to the fullest: to strain your consciousness to feel what the deer are thinking today, this moment; to sit still and let your self go into the birds and wind while waiting by a game trail. Hunting magic is designed to bring the game to you—the creature who has heard your song, witnessed your sincerity, and out of compassion comes within your range. Hunting magic is not only aimed at bringing beasts to their death, but to assist in their birth—to promote their fertility. Thus the great Iberian cave paintings are not of hunting alone—but of animals mating and giving birth. A Spanish farmer who saw some reproductions from Altamira is reported to have said, "How beautifully this cow gives birth to a calf!" Breuil has said, "The religion of those days did *not* elevate the animal to the position of a god . . . but it was *humbly entreated* to be fertile." A Haida incantation goes:

120

"The Great One coming up against the current
    begins thinking of it.
The Great One coming putting gravel in his mouth
    thinks of it
You look at it with white stone eyes—
    Great Eater begins thinking of it."

People of primitive cultures appreciate animals as other
people off on various trips. Snakes move without limbs, and
are like free penises. Birds fly, sing, and dance; they gather food
for their babies; they disappear for months and then come back.
Fish can breathe water and are brilliant colors. Mammals are
like us, they fuck and give birth to babies while panting and
purring; their young suck their mothers' breasts; they know
terror and delight, they play.

Lévi-Strauss quotes Swanton's report on the Chickasaw, the
tribe's own amusing game of seeing the different clans as acting
out the lives of their totemic emblems: "The Raccoon people
were said to live on fish and wild fruit, those of the Puma lived
in the mountains, avoided water of which they were very
frightened and lived principally on game. The Wild Cat clan
slept in the daytime and hunted at night, for they had keen eyes;
they were indifferent to women. Members of the Bird clan were
up before daybreak: 'They were like real birds in that they
would not bother anybody . . . the people of this clan have
different sorts of minds, just as there are different species of
birds.' They were said to live well, to be polygamous, disinclined
to work, and prolific . . . the inhabitants of the 'bending-post-oak'
house group lived in the woods . . . the High Corncrib house
people were respected in spite of their arrogance: they were
good gardeners, very industrious but poor hunters; they
bartered their maize for game. They were said to be truthful and
stubborn, and skilled at forecasting the weather. As for the
Redskunk house group: they lived in dugouts underground."

We all know what primitive cultures don't have. What they
do have is this knowledge of connection and responsibility
which amounts to a spiritual ascesis for the whole community.

Monks of Christianity or Buddhism, "leaving the world" (which means the games of society) are trying, in a decadent way, to achieve what whole primitive communities—men, women, and children—live by daily; and with more wholeness. The Shaman-poet is simply the man whose mind reaches easily out into all manners of shapes and other lives, and gives song to dreams. Poets have carried this function forward all through civilized times: poets don't sing about society, they sing about nature—even if the closest they ever get to nature is their lady's queynt. Class-structured civilized society is a kind of mass ego. To transcend the ego is to go beyond society as well. "Beyond" there lies, inwardly, the unconscious. Outwardly, the equivalent of the unconscious is the wilderness: both of these terms meet, one step even farther on, as *one*.

One religious tradition of this communion with nature which has survived into historic Western times is what has been called Witchcraft. The antlered and pelted figure painted on the cave wall of Trois Frères, a shaman-dancer-poet, is a prototype of both Shiva and the Devil.

Animal marriages (and supernatural marriages) are a common motif of folklore the world around. A recent article by Lynn White puts the blame for the present ecological crisis on the Judaeo-Christian tradition—animals don't have souls and can't be saved; nature is merely a ground for us to exploit while working out our drama of free will and salvation under the watch of Jehovah. The Devil? "The Deivill apeired vnto her in the liknes of ane prettie boy in grein clothes . . . and at that tyme the Deivil gaive hir his markis; and went away from her in the liknes of ane blak dowg." "He wold haw carnall dealling with ws in the shap of a deir, or in any vther shap, now and then, somtyme he vold be lyk a stirk, a bull, a deir, a rae, or a dowg, etc, and haw dealling with us."

The archaic and primitive ritual dramas, which acknowledged all the sides of human nature, including the destructive, demonic, and ambivalent, were liberating and harmonizing. Freud said *he* didn't discover the unconscious, poets had centuries before. The purpose of California Shamanism was "to heal disease and resist death, with a power acquired from dreams." An Arapaho dancer of the Ghost Dance came back from his trance to sing:

"I circle around, I circle around

The boundaries of the earth,
The boundaries of the earth

Wearing the long wing feathers as I fly
Wearing the long wing feathers as I fly."

The Voice as a Girl

"Everything was alive—the trees, grasses, and winds were dancing with me, talking with me; I could understand the songs of the birds." This ancient experience is not so much—in spite of later commentators—"religious" as it is a pure perception of beauty. The phenomenal world experienced at certain pitches is totally living, exciting, mysterious, filling one with a trembling awe, leaving one grateful and humble. The wonder of the mystery returns direct to one's own senses and consciousness: inside and outside; the voice breathes, "Ah!"

Breath is the outer world coming into one's body. With pulse —the two always harmonizing—the source of our inward sense of rhythm. Breath is spirit, "inspiration." Expiration, "voiced," makes the signals by which the species connects. Certain emotions and states occasionally seize the body, one becomes a whole tube of air vibrating; all voice. In mantra chanting, the magic utterances, built of seed-syllables such as OM and AYNG and AH, repeated over and over, fold and curl on the breath until—when most weary and bored—a new voice enters, a voice speaks through you clearer and stronger than what you know of yourself; with a sureness and melody of its own, singing out the inner song of the self, and of the planet.

123

Poetry, it should not have to be said, is not writing or books. Non-literate cultures with their traditional training methods of hearing and reciting, carry thousands of poems—death, war, love, dream, work, and spirit-power songs—through time. The voice of inspiration as an "other" has long been known in the West as The Muse. Widely speaking, the muse is anything other that touches you and moves you. Be it a mountain range, a band of people, the morning star, or a diesel generator. Breaks through the ego-barrier. But this touching-deep is as a mirror, and man in his sexual nature has found the clearest mirror to be his human lover. As the West moved into increasing complexities and hierarchies with civilization, Woman as nature, beauty, and The Other came to be an all-dominating symbol; secretly striving through the last three millennia with the Jehovah or Imperator God-figure, a projection of the gathered power of anti-nature social forces. Thus in the Western tradition the Muse and Romantic Love became part of the same energy, and woman as nature the field for experiencing the universe as sacramental. The lovers bed was the sole place to enact the dances and ritual dramas that link primitive people to their geology and the Milky Way. The contemporary decline of the cult of romance is linked to the rise of the sense of the primitive, and the knowledge of the variety of spiritual practices and paths to beauty that cultural anthropology has brought us. We begin to move away now, in this interesting historical spiral, from monogamy and monotheism.

Yet the muse remains a woman. Poetry is voice, and according to Indian tradition, voice, vāk (vox)—is a Goddess. Vāk is also called Sarasvati, she is the lover of Brahma and his actual creative energy; she rides a peacock, wears white, carries a book-scroll and a vīna. The name Sarasvati means "the flowing one." "She is again the Divine in the aspect of wisdom and learning, for she is the Mother of Veda; that is of all knowledge touching Brahman and the universe. She is the Word of which it was born and She is that which is the issue of her great womb, Mahāyoni. Not therefore idly have men worshipped Vāk, or Sarasvati, as the Supreme Power."

As Vāk is wife to Brahma ("wife" means "wave" means "vibrator" in Indo-European etymology) so the voice, in everyone, is a mirror of his own deepest self. The voice rises to answer an inner need; or as BusTon says, "The voice of the Buddha arises, being called forth by the thought of the living beings." In esoteric Buddhism this becomes the basis of a mandala meditation practice: "In their midst is Nayika, the essence of *Ali,* the vowel series—she possesses the true nature of Vajrasattva, and is Queen of the Vajra-realm. She is known as the Lady, as Suchness, as Void, as Perfection of Wisdom, as limit of Reality, as Absence of Self."

The conch shell is an ancient symbol of the sense of hearing, and of the female; the vulva and the fruitful womb. At Koptos there is a bas-relief of a four-point buck, on the statue of the god Min, licking his tongue out toward two conches. There are many Magdalenian bone and horn engravings of bear, bison, and deer licking abstract penises and vulvas. At this point (and from our most archaic past transmitted) the mystery of voice becomes one with the mystery of body.

How does this work among primitive peoples in practice? James Mooney, discussing the Ghost Dance religion, says "There is no limit to the number of these [Ghost Dance] songs, as every trance at every dance produces a new one, the trance subject after regaining consciousness embodying his experience in the spirit world in the form of a song, which is sung at the next dance and succeeding performances until superseded by other songs originating in the same way. Thus a single dance may easily result in twenty or thirty new songs. While songs are thus born and die, certain ones which appeal especially to the Indian heart, on account of their mythology, pathos, or peculiar sweetness, live and are perpetuated."

Modern poets in America, Europe, and Japan, are discovering the breath, the voice, and trance. It is also for some a discovery to realize that the universe is not a dead thing but a continual creation, the song of Sarasvati springing from the trance of Brahma. "Reverence to Her who is eternal, Raudrī, Gaurī, Dhātri, reverence and again reverence, to Her who is the Consciousness in all beings, reverence and again reverence. . . . Candī says."

Hopscotch and Cats Cradles

> The clouds are "Shining Heaven" with his different bird-blankets on
>
> —Haida

The human race, as it immediately concerns us, has a vertical axis of about 40,000 years and as of 1900 AD a horizonal spread of roughly 3000 different languages and 1000 different cultures. Every living culture and language is the result of countless cross-fertilizations—not a "rise and fall" of civilizations, but more like a flowerlike periodic absorbing—blooming—bursting and scattering of seed. Today we are aware as never before of the plurality of human life-styles and possibilities, while at the same time being tied, like in an old silent movie, to a runaway locomotive rushing headlong toward a very singular catastrophe. Science, as far as it is capable of looking "on beauty bare" is on our side. Part of our being modern is the very fact of our awareness that we are one with our beginnings—contemporary with all periods—members of all cultures. The seeds of every social structure or custom are in the mind.

The anthropologist Stanley Diamond has said "The sickness of civilization consists in its failure to incorporate (and only then) to move beyond the limits of the primitive." Civilization is so to speak a lack of faith, a human laziness, a willingness to accept the perceptions and decisions of others in place of your own—to be less than a full man. Plus, perhaps, a primate inheritance of excessive socializing; and surviving submission/

dominance traits (as can be observed in monkey or baboon bands) closely related to exploitative sexuality. If evolution has any meaning at all we must hope to slowly move away from such biological limitations, just as it is within our power to move away from the self-imposed limitations of small-minded social systems. We all live within skin, ego, society, and species boundaries. Consciousness has boundaries of a different order, "the mind is free." College students trying something different because "they do it in New Guinea" is part of the real work of modern man: to uncover the inner structure and actual boundaries of the mind. The third Mystery. The charts and maps of this realm are called mandalas in Sanskrit. (A poem by the Sixth Dalai Lama runs "Drawing diagrams I measured / Movement of the stars / Though her tender flesh is near / Her mind I cannot measure.") Buddhist and Hindu philosophers have gone deeper into this than almost anyone else but the work is just beginning. We are now gathering all the threads of history together and linking modern science to the primitive and archaic sources.

The stability of certain folklore motifs and themes— evidences of linguistic borrowing—the deeper meaning of linguistic drift—the laws by which styles and structures, art-forms and grammars, songs and ways of courting, relate and reflect each other are all mirrors of the self. Even the uses of the word "nature," as in the seventeenth-century witch Isobel Gowdie's testimony about what it was like to make love to the Devil—"I found his nature cold within me as spring-well-water" —throw light on human nature.

Thus nature leads into nature—the wilderness—and the reciprocities and balances by which man lives on earth. Ecology: "eco" (*oikos*) meaning "house" (cf. "ecumenical"): Housekeeping on Earth. Economics, which is merely the housekeeping of various social orders—taking out more than it puts back—must learn the rules of the greater realm. Ancient and primitive cultures had this knowledge more surely and with almost as much empirical precision (see H. C. Conklin's work on Hanunoo plant-knowledge, for example) as the most concerned biologist today. Inner and outer: the Brihadāranyaka Upanishad says, "Now this Self is the state of being of all contingent beings. In so far as a man pours libations and offers sacrifice, he is in the sphere of the gods; in so far as he recites the Veda he is in the sphere of the seers; in so far as he offers cakes and water to the ancestors, in so far as he gives food and lodging to men, he is of the sphere of men. In so far as he finds grass and water for domestic animals, he is in the sphere of domestic animals; in so far as wild beasts and birds, even down to ants, find something to live on in his house, he is of their sphere."

The primitive world view, far-out scientific knowledge and the poetic imagination are related forces which may help if not to save the world or humanity, at least to save the Redwoods. The goal of Revolution is Transformation. Mystical traditions within the great religions of civilized times have taught a doctrine of Great Effort for the achievement of Transcendence. This must have been their necessary compromise with civilization, which needed for its period to turn man's vision away from nature, to nourish the growth of the social energy. The archaic, the esoteric, and the primitive traditions alike all teach that beyond transcendence is Great Play, and Transformation. After the mind-breaking Void, the emptiness of a million universes appearing and disappearing, all created things rushing into Krishna's devouring mouth; beyond the enlightenment that can say "these beings are dead already; go ahead and kill them, Arjuna" is a loving, simple awareness of the absolute beauty and preciousness of mice and weeds.

Tsong-kha-pa tells us of a transformed universe:
"1. This is a Buddha-realm of infinite beauty
 2. All men are divine, are subjects
 3. Whatever we use or own are vehicles of worship
 4. All acts are authentic, not escapes."

Such authenticity is at the heart of many a primitive world view. For the Anaguta of the Jos plateau, Northern Nigeria,

North is called "up"; South is called "down." East is called "morning" and West is called "evening." Hence (according to Dr. Stanley Diamond in his *Anaguta Cosmography*), "Time flows past the permanent central position . . . they live at a place called noon, at the center of the world, the only place where space and time intersect." The Australian aborigines live in a world of ongoing recurrence—comradeship with the landscape and continual exchanges of being and form and position; every person, animals, forces, all are related via a web of reincarnation—or rather, they are "interborn." It may well be that rebirth (or interbirth, for we are actually mutually creating each other and all things while living) is the objective fact of existence which we have not yet brought into conscious knowledge and practice.

It is clear that the empirically observable interconnectedness of nature is but a corner of the vast "jewelled net" which moves from without to within. The spiral (think of nebulae) and spiral conch (vulva/womb) is a symbol of the Great Goddess. It is charming to note that physical properties of spiral conches approximate the Indian notion of the world-creating dance, "expanding form"—"We see that the successive chambers of a spiral Nautilus or of a straight Orthoceras, each whorl or part of a whorl of a periwinkle or other gastropod, each additional increment of an elephant's tusk, or each new chamber of a spiral foraminifer, has its leading characteristic at once described and its form so far described by the simple statement that it constitutes a *gnomon* to the whole previously existing structure." (D'Arcy Thompson.)

The maze dances, spiral processions, cats cradles, Micronesian string star-charts, mandalas and symbolic journeys of the old wild world are with us still in the universally distributed childrens' game. Let poetry and Bushmen lead the way in a great hop forward:

"In the following game of long hopscotch, the part marked H is for Heaven: it is played in the usual way except that when you are finishing the first part, on the way up, you throw

your tor into Heaven. Then you hop to 11, pick up your tor,
jump to the very spot where your tor landed in Heaven,
and say, as fast as you can,
the alphabet forwards and backwards,
your name, address and telephone number (if you have one),
your age,
and the name of your boyfriend or girl-friend (if you have
one of those)." (Patricia Evans, *Hopscotch*)

XII. '67

DHARMA QUERIES

A Quick Review of the Present Yuga

1.　Nature and Man—the great Paleolithic Goddess and the antler'd dancer—magic paintings in caves; red hands; red dots.

2.　Social Energy and Man—the gathering of bronze and iron-age power; tribes become "nations" and expand—the Pole Star, the War Chief, and the penis-as-weapon resolve as God in Heaven.

3.　A reaction to pure social and warrior-power mystiques: teachers of social management—Confucius, Zoroaster, Judaic reforms; spiritual-social disciplines like the *Gīta*.

4.　Christianity, Buddhism, Confucianism, temper the power hunger of states and castles; with emphasis on individual responsibility and liberation.

5.　These systems become power-manipulators in turn, while within them survivals of archaic Nature-and-Man traditions regain influence. Yogacara Buddhism leading toward Vajrayāna; Mediterranean mystery cults leading toward dozens of occidental occult and alchemical streams of thought.

6.　Contemporary science: the knowledge that society and any given cultural outlook is arbitrary; and that the more we conquer Nature the weaker we get. The objective eye of science, striving to see Nature plain, must finally look at "subject" and "object" and the very Eye that looks. We discover that all

131

of us carry within us caves; with animals and gods on the walls; a place of ritual and magic.

The Buddha as Son and Lover of the Goddess

Born of *Maya* who dreamed of an *elephant*—and gave birth to him standing, in the posture of a *Yakshi* holding a limb and giving a fertility-kick to a *tree;* husband to a beautiful princess and many wives; cut off his *hair;* and underwent *austerities;* when near death brought *yogurt* by a *girl,* which restored him; near a *river;* sat in the *lotus* posture under a *fig* tree; was tempted by the daughters of Mara; saw the *Morning Star* and had an enlightenment of which the content was a total comprehension of the nature of *interdependent co-creation;* called the *Earth Goddess* to witness, was protected and hailed by *Serpent Kings* and pelted with *flowers* by Devas; spent his remaining years wandering and teaching the way to the *other shore;* died after eating a *mushroom;* and was grieved over by countless humans, gods, and *wild animals.*

The Real Old Goodspell

Buddhism and Hinduism carry much of the Stone Age religion along with them. Shaving the head: sacrifice of the body (or self-castration, as in ancient Anatolia)—an offering of one's "natural power" to the Goddess. (The earliest shaved heads I've found so far: illustrations of a "temple

132

dairy farm" at the neolithic temple site of Al 'Ubaid: "the
Goddess of the pastures was herself the Cow"—the frieze shows
"all the stages in the preparation of her milk, by men whose
shorn heads mark them as priests . . . ." G. R. Levy)

Types of relation to the Goddess: the Bhikku or ascetic:
"I'll shave my head and be your servant if you'll save me."
Zen: "We shall be equals, and I'll ignore you." Tantrism:
"I'll give you all my loving."

To follow the ancient path in company with a lover means
both must have practiced the lonely yogas and wanderings,
and then seek the center of the individual-body and group-body
mandala; dedicating their two loving bodies to the whole
network; the man evoking the Goddess in the girl on suitable
occasions and worshiping her. She is his mudrā, prajñā,
yoginī, or spell (vidyā).

Long hair is to accept, go *through* the powers of nature. Such
are the Shaivite yokins; or the Kagyü-pa and Nyinma-pa
lamas; the ancient Rishis. I knew a Wasco Indian logger (a
faller) who quit logging (Warm Springs Camp A) and sold his
chainsaw because he said he couldn't stand hearing the trees
scream as he cut into them. He apprenticed himself to an
old shaman and let his hair grow long.

Gods and Bodhisattvas we see in men and woman, who are
they?

It appears there actually is some sort of reincarnation.

Something long range is taking place; in each individual
—sometimes—behind the mask of *this* foolish person, *this*
foolish lifetime, we see the Bodhisattva-figure who is both
brilliance and compassion working for all beings. In all of us.

"Having finished his time as a Zen Master he has proceeded
on to the next phase of his training." Miura Rōshi told me
that even Śhākyamuni is still working on himself somewhere.

The Goddess "Māyā" (measure/illusion) and "Gone-beyond
Wisdom" (Prajñāpāramitā, Mother of the Buddhas) are one.
In her and holding her (dhṛ—uphold>*dharma*) is the Adi-
Buddha Dharmakāya / Vajradhara / Vairocana; *thus come.*

133

The Dharma is this embrace; the energy of all being is
this bliss:

/ acting out the present kalpa through Amitābha
through Avalokiteśvara through Śākyamuni through *you*.

next:

Sometimes it is possible to cut crosswise the time-stream
of rebirths—the grand plans and dances, eschatologies and
evolutions; and be *now:* [the "marvelous emptiness" in all
possibilities and directions. Which embraces the game of time
and evolution.

then:

To return to the play with the work of making it for the
"time" or future time, Beautiful. Flowers for the Void.
Compassion and dignity—done for beings that don't *really* need
it. "I have a sentimental attachment to the wild ecologies."
The re-enactment of a timeless dance: [here and now, co-creating
forever, for no end but now.

thus the vow.

—but enough of this wild fox barking.

OM   MANI   PADME   HUM

SUWA-NO-SE ISLAND
AND THE BANYAN
ASHRAM

Several years ago Nanao SAKAKI, the wanderer and poet,
was traveling on a small interisland freighter between Kyushu
and Amami Oshima and got into a conversation with a fellow
passenger, an islander, who casually invited Nanao to come visit
his island. Nanao did, another year, and just when a typhoon
came; so he was holed up for over a week in a farmhouse
waiting for the storm to blow over.

The island has only eight households—forty people—and,
though the major part of the island is volcano and lavaflow, there
is plenty of unoccupied land that is livable. Hence the islanders
told Nanao that if he or his friends wished to come camp or
live there, they'd be welcome.

Nanao's old circle of friends in Tokyo, the "Emerald Breeze"
branch of the "Harijan" (formerly known as the Bum Academy)
had already started a farm in the highlands of Nagano
prefecture. They decided to add Suwa-no-se Island to their
plans: In May, Nanao, Miko and Shinkai went down; Pon in
June with several others; Franco, Naga, Masa, and me in July.
You have to go to Kagoshima, the southernmost town of size in
Kyushu. A boat leaves for the "Ten Islands" once a week.
Unpredictably. So that we were hung up for five days in
Kagoshima, a cheap waterfront inn, while the ship waited out a
typhoon scare. Did our grocery shopping and walked out
to the ends of breakwaters waiting.

The "Toshima Maru" left at six in the evening. A little diesel

freighter of 250 tons. At daybreak coming in on Kuchi-no-erabu
Island—silvery rainsqualls, green cliffs, flashings of seabirds.
The ship called at three islands through the day—anchoring
beyond the edge of the coral reef, loading and unloading
from tossing little unpainted island boats.

Late in the afternoon the ship was approaching Suwa-no-se,
a violet mountain from afar, with cloudcaps and banners of
mist. (The fishermen who come down from Miyazaki on Kyushu
in their seaworthy little 3 ton fishing boats call it "Yake-jima"
—Burning Island. Because much of the time the volcano is
smoking.)

Anchoring offshore, the "Toshima Maru" blows its whistle
and finally, down a steep trail through bamboo, a few men
running. After half an hour a small boat puts out from
behind a big boulder and cement breakwater at the base of the
cliffs—steers through a path in the coral reef and comes
alongside the freighter. The islanders brought out watermelons
and wild goats. The goats go down to Amami Oshima where
people like to eat them. Then, us, with our rucksacks and
provisions, aboard the little boat, ashore through rough waves
and getting wet, up on the rocky beach. Stepping over and
through the lines and cables of several small fishing boats, nets,
cables of the winch system for handling the boats in and out.
Everybody waiting for us, almost black from being always in the
sun. Packed all our groceries and rucksacks up the switchbacks
and across a mile or so of trail through semijungle to the
abandoned house and clearing they were using. Nanao and
Shinkai had just finished a small extra shelter of bamboo;
dome-shaped, with a thatch roof—so there was sleeping space
for everyone. Fourteen people, almost half of them girls.

Suwa-no-se is latitude 29° 36′, which puts it on a level
roughly with the Canary Islands, Cairo, Chihuahua, Persepolis
and Lhasa. Almost halfway from Kyushu to Amami Oshima.
The Amami group of islands continue into the Ryukyus
and the culture is quite similar to the Okinawan but there are
dialect differences. From Yoron Island you can see Okinawa they

say. Yoron is part of Japan. Suwa-no-se was probably populated off and on for several thousand years, depending on the activity of the volcano. The "Ten Islands" are part of a steppingstone system of islands all the way from Taiwan to Kyushu, by which paleolithic voyagers worked their way up to Japan. So they must have stopped off. Suwa-no-se was abandoned after the great eruption of the 15th Century, and nobody returned until a century ago when some settlers came up from Amami to try again. Our villagers are thus of the Amami line, and speak Amami dialect; play the snake-head "jabisen" instead of the catskin-head "shamisen." They keep pigs, which is also an Amami custom. Mainland Japanese have never much taken to pigs. Also, they drink distilled sweet-potato liquor instead of sake; and sweet potatoes make a main part of the year's food—cheaper and easier to raise on the windy islands than rice.

The main part of the island is mountainous and uninhabited, but there is a kind of plateau about 400 feet above sea level that makes a southern extension, with several good streams running through it—an arable plateau maybe two miles by three miles, and covered for the most part by bamboo and grasses. A great pasture of fifty or so acres toward the east, and some pine and *Tabu* forests on the flanks of the mountain. Banyan trees and other large subtropical plants follow in the watercourses.

Sweet-potato and watermelon fields are cut-out squares in the bamboo here and there. The houses are clustered toward the west, which is closest to the little harbor; each house separate and enclosed in a wall of bamboo. Even the trails are shadowy corridors through the bamboo jungle and under the limbs of the banyan.

In the open pasture twenty-three head of black beef cattle at large, and on the edge of the pasture the abandoned farmhouse that became our headquarters. Up the meadow a way toward the mountain is a magnificent banyan on the edge of a ravine— we cleared out a meditation ground within its hanging roots

—finally called our whole place "Banyan Ashram," or Pon calls it "Banyan Dream."

Daily work was clearing a new field for sweet-potato planting. We had to get all the bamboo root runners out, turning it over with hoes and grubbing the roots. Backbreaking work, and very slow. Because of midday heat it could only be done before 10:30 or after 4. In midday we napped in the shade of the banyan, or in the Bamboo House. Other work was fuel-gathering (dead pine underbranches; dead bamboo; or driftwood from the beaches loaded in a carrying basket and toted with a tumpline on the forehead) and cooking; done by turn in pairs in an open kitchen-shed with a thatch roof on an old brick campfire stove. Chinese style. (Our diet was basically brown rice and miso soup with potatoes and sweet potatoes and occasional watermelons or local bananas.) Also a lot of carpentry and construction work was continually going on, and a few hands every few days down to the village to join in on a village project, community trail-repair, or helping gut and flay an extra-large flying fish catch before it could spoil.

The ocean: every day except when the wind was too strong (fringe of a typhoon somewhere) most of us made it to the beach. There are three places to go: the eastern beach, forty minutes by trail, is wide and rough, with a good view of the volcano. The waves are very heavy. It looks across the Pacific toward Mexico. The coral reef goes out a long way, so it's not suitable for skindiving except when the weather is exceptionally calm. The beach has splendid driftwood and drift-lumber, and lots of seashells to gather. There's a cave toward one end within which thirty-six cows can stand in a rainstorm without getting wet. The southern beach is reached by a brushy trail also forty minutes—steep descent down the cliff but possible no-hands; it has a shorter coral ledge and a lovely natural cove within the coral which is deep and affords a passage into deep water under the breakers (i.e., you swim out to the gate and dive and glide underwater for thirty or forty feet and surface beyond the heavy pounding). There are strong

138

tidal currents here, and we decided it was dangerous for
anyone not an excellent swimmer and diver.

The western beach is the most sheltered and the best for
fishing. We had vague ideas about spearfishing from the
beginning and I brought a pocketful of steel harpoon heads
(the smallest ones) with me—but it wasn't until Arikawa-san,
the youngest family man of the islanders, showed us how to
make a long bamboo spear with an iron rod in the end on which
the spearhead sockets (attached to the main bamboo by
leader) that we seriously began to think about adding fish to our
diet. The spear is powered by inner-tube rubber, and is about
nine feet long. Ito and I made three of these. With flippers
and goggles, spent two fruitless days in the water 'til we began
to understand the habits and feelings of the different species.
Then we began to take them regularly. It became noticeably
easier to do heavy work with more protein in the diet.

Most of us would be vegetarians by choice, but this was a real
case of necessity and ecology. The volcanic soil of the island
(and the volcanic ash fallout) makes it hard to raise many
vegetables there; but the waters are rich in fish. We offered our
respects and gratitude to the fish and the Sea Gods daily,
and ate them with real love, admiring their extraordinarily
beautiful, perfect little bodies.

Hundreds of varieties and thousands of individuals, all edible.
Cobalt blue, shades of yellow and orange seemed the most
common. None of the fish are really "tropical" and strange—
but they are clearly subtropical with more variety than you'd
find in colder waters. I became absorbed in the life of the
sea. Without a fish book I came to recognize dozens of species
and gradually came to know their habits and peculiarities
and territories and emotions.

There is a great truth in the relationship established by
hunting: like in love or art, you must become one with the
other. (Which is why paleolithic hunting magic is so important
historically: the necessities of identity, intuition, stillness, that
go with hunting make it seem as though shamanism and yoga

139

and meditation may have their roots in the requirements of the hunter—where a man learns to be motionless for a day, putting his mind in an open state so that his consciousness won't spook creatures that he knows will soon be approaching.)

In spearfishing we learned you must never choose a specific fish for a quarry: you must let the fish choose you, and be prepared to shoot the fish that will come into range. For some fish you must be one with the sea and consider yourself a fish among fish. But there was one large and unpredictable variety (cobalt with a crescent-shaped tail) that digs the strange. When one of those was around I would change my mind and consider myself a freak and be out of place; in which case he will come to look at you out of curiosity.

When you go down with the fishes minus your spear they treat you differently too. I got so I could go down to twenty-five or thirty feet fairly comfortably. An old man originally from Okinawa, Uaji-san, dives sixty feet. He's seventy years old, and has a wise, tough, beautiful young wife. He caught a sea turtle and gave most of it to the Ashram once.

Sometimes the islanders had special catches on their little boats; once we had all the shark meat we could eat; another time a giant feast of raw sawara; once a whole bucket of flying-fish eggs. A few times went on shellfish-gathering expeditions together. By next summer the Ashram plans to have a small boat, which will make fishing a regular and efficient operation.

The weather is breezy, the sun hot. The ocean sends up great squalls and sudden rainstorms which dry up in twenty minutes. The volcano goes grummmmmmmm and lots of purple smoke comes up, into the sky, to 15,000 feet.

Meals were served on the mat-floor of the farmhouse, everybody crosslegged, with Taku-chan the Gotos' two-year-old boy wandering stark naked through it all. After supper at night we generally sat almost totally silent around our two or three candles, sometimes humming mantras or folksongs; or went out in the cow pasture with a bottle of shochu and played the jew's-harp (which the Harijan all call a bigigi, the New Guinea name for it) and the Kenya drum (a present from Ginzap four years ago) to our patron star, Antares.

Those whose rose very early went to meditate under the banyan—a lovely thing especially because of the song of the Akahige ("Redbeard" Temminck's Robin) which sings in the early-morning canyons with a remarkable trilling, falling song that drops three octaves and echoes across hills and meadows. Also the songs of the Hototo-gisu (Himalayan Cuckoo) and Blue Doves—filling up the whole morning world with song. While morning mists blow and curl around and the grass is all dewy and the Rising Sun of Japan comes up through the ocean and the fog like a big red rising sun flag.

After breakfast every morning there would be a quiet, natural discussion of the day's work; people would volunteer for various tasks—never any pressuring—somebody might say, "Let's be sure and put the tools back where we got them, I couldn't find the file yesterday" or something—but without acrimony; Westerners have much to learn from this easy cooperativeness and sense of getting the work done without fuss. The Banyan people had less ego-friction (none!) and difficulty over chores than any group I've ever seen.

Masa UEHARA and I were married on the island on August 6, the new moon. The whole ashram stayed up late the night before, packing a breakfast for the morrow—and broiling a splendid pink tai that was a present from the village. (No marriage is complete if you don't eat tai afterwards, the noble, calm AUSPICIOUS FISH of Japan.) We got up at 4:30 and started up the brush trail in the dark. First dipping into a ravine and then winding up a jungly knife-edge ridge. By five we were out of the jungle and onto a bare lava slope. Following the long ridge to an older, extinct crater, and on to the crest of the main crater and the summit shortly after sunrise. The lip of the crater drops off into cloud; and out of the cloud comes a roaring like an airport full of jets: a billowing of steam upwards. The cloud and mist broke, and we could see 800 feet or so down into the crater—at least a mile across—and fumaroles and steam-jets; at the very center red molten lava in a little bubbly pond. The noise, according to the switch of the wind, sometimes deafening.

Standing on the edge of the crater, blowing the conch horn and chanting a mantra; offering shochu to the gods of the volcano, the ocean, and the sky; then Masa and I exchanged the traditional three sips—Pon and Nanao said a few words; Masa and I spoke; we recited the Four Vows together, and ended with three blasts on the conch. Got out of the wind and opened the rucksacks to eat the food made the night before, and drink the rest of the shochu. We descended from the summit and were down to the Banyan tree by eleven—went direct on out to the ocean and into the water; so that within one morning we passed from the windy volcanic summit to the warm coral waters. At four in the afternoon all the villagers came to the Ashram—we served saké and shochu—pretty soon everyone was singing Amami folksongs and doing traditional dances.

The sweet-potato field got cleared and planted; Franco left a bit early to be in San Luis Obispo by mid-September; we started clearing another patch of land and built a big outdoor table of driftwood; went around to the north side of the island in a small boat to investigate other possibilities of settlements and fishing.

Masa and I caught the "Toshima Maru" heading on south at the end of August and visited Cho in Koniya; with Shinkai checked on boatbuilders' prices; took another ship up to Kagoshima (all night on the deck sitting on matting watching the full moon).

And hitchhiked to Miyazaki for a three-day Harijan gathering and a look at the neolithic tumuli in the region; and back to Kyoto. Miko and Akibananda and others will be on the island all year; Pon and Nanao are back up in Nagano at the mountain Ashram now.

It is possible at last for Masa and me to imagine a little of what the ancient—archaic—mind and life of Japan were. And to see what could be restored to the life today. A lot of it is simply in being aware of clouds and wind.

Eighth Moon, 40067
(*reckoning roughly from the earliest cave paintings*)